ADOBE® MASTER CLASS
ILLUSTRATOR®

INSPIRING ARTWORK AND TUTORIALS BY ESTABLISHED AND EMERGING ARTISTS

ADOBE
PRESS

Adobe

ADOBE® MASTER CLASS: ILLUSTRATOR®
Inspiring artwork and tutorials by established and emerging artists
Curated by Sharon Milne

This Adobe Press book is published by Peachpit, a division of Pearson Education.

For the latest on Adobe Press books, go to
www.adobepress.com

To report errors, please send a note to: errata@peachpit.com

Acquisitions and Project Editor: Rebecca Gulick
Developmental Editors: Rebecca Gulick and Liz Welch
Copy Editor: Liz Welch
Production Coordinator: Becky Winter
Cover Design: Charlene Charles-Will
Interior Design and Compositing: Charlene Charles-Will and Kim Scott, Bumpy Design
Cover Images: Nabhan Abdullatif, Justin Currie, Ekaterina Dedova, Maria Goubar, Grelin Machin, Svetlana Makarova, Sharon Milne, Michelle Romo

ISBN-13: 978-0-321-88640-8
ISBN-10: 0-321-88640-2

9 8 7 6 5 4 3 2 1
Printed and bound in the United States of America

For Paul and the girls: Sam, Shelley, and Super Harls.

You keep me sane and always loved.

ADOBE MASTER CLASS **ILLUSTRATOR**

For some artists and designers, facing the blank canvas of a new Adobe Illustrator document is an intimidating challenge. But viewing the astonishing and inspiring work that Sharon Milne has curated for this Adobe Press *Master Class* book on Illustrator, it's clear to me that others relish and revel in the creative freedom offered by that open, white canvas and the creative tools at their disposal in Illustrator.

It's such a pleasure for me to write this foreword. Sharon Milne is a true friend of the Illustrator and vector graphics communities. Sharon, whose own creativity and considerable Illustrator skills are matched by her generosity in sharing her techniques and insights with others, has brought together artists from around the world whose work exudes energy, imagination, and passion, along with an impressive mastery of technique. Colorful and happy, elegant and pure, or dark and expressive, each artist is sure to inspire and delight you with his or her remarkable creative vision.

It's my hope that this inspiration continues as these artists share their Illustrator workflows in the detailed tutorials in this book. Learn new ways to capture your own creative vision with the intricate shapes, expressive color, complex effects, and rich typography that are waiting for you to explore in Illustrator.

So embrace that wide-open canvas in Illustrator and the creative freedom it represents. Remember, with vector, you're always on a path that's going somewhere.

—Terry Hemphill
   Senior Product Marketing Manager
   Adobe Illustrator

When Adobe launched Illustrator in 1987, the key factor was that designers could create crisp illustrations and logos using *vectors*. Illustrator creates graphics based on mathematical paths and points, so artwork is infinitely scalable. Imagine that! A logo that can literally be printed the size of a billboard without any pixilation—the edges remain the same high quality just as if it were sized at 100%!

Now I confess, when all of this started, I didn't even know what a computer was. I was still messing with pencils and rolls of wallpaper on my mother's carpet. It wasn't until about 10 years ago I discovered vector art and what it was capable of. At the time, I thought of vector art as being something similar to a cartoon-styled graphic, similar to cel shading.

When I ventured into digital art, I wrestled with what size to have my digital canvas. I wanted to make it large so I could have a high-quality piece to print, but it took up so much space on my hard drive and rendered so slowly. So when I learned about the scalable properties of vector art created in Illustrator, my mind was truly blown. When vector came along in my life, I realized size was something I no longer had to worry about. This is one of the things that make vector such an appealing medium.

With each new version of Adobe Illustrator, great new tools and options are introduced, advancing artists from basic color vector graphics in 1987 to creating digital painted artwork, with the advent of Bristle Brush in Illustrator CS5 and Gradients and Strokes in Illustrator CS6. Tools such as Gradient Mesh give the skilled graphic designer the ability to create smooth vector graphics that look like an airbrushed digital painting! With the introduction of Live Trace, which later was replaced in Illustrator CS6 by Image Trace, you can push the medium even further and trace a photograph, color for color, and create a scalable image with realistic detail.

The benefits of Illustrator are not only infinite scalability, but also versatility that can't be matched with raster graphics. What may take hours in a raster image can be done in Adobe Illustrator with a few clicks. That means your client could request color or shape changes at the eleventh hour, and you could effortlessly modify the graphic to their new specifications.

However, there is some trade-off to all these benefits of the medium. As it's all based on mathematical points and paths, if you want to create awesome vector-based paintings, it takes skill, creativity, and a lot of planning! It can be much easier to create that appearance in a raster-based program, if you're willing to sacrifice the versatility of vector. So who's willing to go through all of that? You'll be happy to know there are phenomenal vector artists out there who continually test the boundaries of the vector medium and Illustrator, proving that creative challenges can make for some very beautiful artwork.

It's my privilege to introduce you to some of these artists.

Adobe Master Class: Illustrator presents 31 artists who use Illustrator to create stylish, innovative, and inspiring illustration work, taking the humble paths and points beyond the logo and mascot to full-fledged works of art. As an active member of the online vector community, I've encountered many talented vector artists. They are part of the amazing art communities of deviantArt and Vectortuts+, as well as Adobe's own Illustrator blog.

Although I consider it a blessing to know nearly all these people, it's made the job of selecting artists to showcase in this book extremely difficult. I've chosen artists who not only create aesthetically pleasing work in various styles, but also are technically impressive. I introduce you to artists who stick to the basic tools and recycle elements throughout their work. They are using the fundamental features of Illustrator to create

amazing images that will make the avid raster artist consider crossing over to the scalable side.

The artists featured here tell you about their inspirations and their relationship with Illustrator, and several of them give you firsthand insights into their process through the book's 11 tutorials.

The inspiring artists you'll meet in these pages push the limits of what can be achieved in Illustrator and help chart the course for this powerful software's continued evolution.

—Sharon Milne
  November 2012

ADOBE® MASTER CLASS
ILLUSTRATOR®

Svetlana Makarova

"Spicing my illustrations with some humor makes my mood better."

◀ RED RIDING HOOD, 2011

I am a Ukrainian self-taught fashion illustrator. I have always been fond of art and fashion, so no wonder this passion of mine has finally led me to what I'm doing now.

In my illustrations I focus on creating appealing and accomplished looks for my exquisite fashion characters, and I make them tell little stories or just strike their poses. I always pay a lot of attention to details, shapes, volume, highlights and shadows, and fabric textures, and I use fresh, vibrant colors. Spicing my illustrations with some humor makes my mood better.

Every new piece is a little self-challenge for me because with every one I set a new goal I want to achieve in the drawing. This could be either some complex shape with many patterns or some specific atmosphere I want the illustration to possess. Being able to express my thoughts and feelings or just tell some funny story with my art—growing professionally with every piece—is a great pleasure for me and an essential part of my life.

▶ SWEET CHILD OF MINE, 2011

Funny Bunny, 2010

Dragon Girl, 2012

◀ Tarot Justice, 2010

ALICE, 2012

Bree Léman

"Illustration brings a very imaginative and natural human touch to a garment."

RUNWAY, 2012

▸ ROMANTIC CHIFFON, 2012

Fashion illustration conveys a specific attitude or mood as a piece of art. I've found that illustration brings a very imaginative and natural human touch to a client's concept/garment. It provides a means of communicating to an audience through an alternative medium that is alive and different.

My fashion-themed portfolio is most aptly described as refined elegance. The women I portray exude confidence in their poses and show whimsical attitudes to the viewer. In essence, my illustrations tell a fashion story. They catch the flowing movement of the garment; every sparkle and ambient light helps create the mood. Oftentimes my themes are illustrated in a whimsical way so that the model, garment, and atmosphere stay in a playful light. I strive to create each design with an eye toward the industry and its followers, while always staying faithful to my true nature. Consistency is also an important goal that I have for my illustrations. Consistency with colors, the sweep of the picture, and the fun nature I try to project into those pieces is paramount to being faithful to myself. My love and respect for fashion is at the heart of everything I illustrate—it's a part of me.

I draw my inspiration from top designers and their runway shows, as well as from my artistic role models who have a true passion for lovely line work and beautiful splashes of color. Some of those artists include Hilda Glasgow, Manuel Rebollo, Grant Cowan, Nuno DaCosta, J.C. Leyendecker, Bec Winnel, Arturo Elena, and Robert McGinnis.

I am thankful for Adobe Illustrator, which lets me conjure the colors, shapes, and scenes needed to achieve my goals and make changes on the fly.

breeleman.com

TEEN FASHION 1, 2011

TEEN FASHION 2, 2011

LACE CORSET, 2012

50's Fashion, 2011

Helen Huang

"I use vector art as the main medium for my fresh, clean style."

FASHION 1, 2010

I see my art as being feminine and elegant. It's a light-hearted and playful mix of high-end fashion and surreal illustration conceptual work. It's often filled with soft pastel palettes and flowing curves. I use vector art as the main medium for my fresh, clean style. I consider Manga, fashion, and my Chinese heritage the major influences on my work.

I am a self-taught digital artist. Art has always been my true passion and motivated me to change my career choice from being a lawyer to a designer. By day I am a full-time designer at an interactive ad agency in Los Angeles, working in Flash, Photoshop, Illustrator, and After Effects. At night I wander in my fantasy art world, trying to capture every inspiration I have and share my vision of the world. My current work focuses on fashion illustration, editorial, and character design. I enjoy sharing my vision with the world and hope my art brings you inspiration and happiness.

▶ WIZARD OF OZ, 2011

HELLO, 2011

REBIRTH, 2010

Matching Outfits, 2012

Love me Love me Not, 2011

Bunny Girl, from Sketch to Finish

In this tutorial I'll show you my workflow in Illustrator for creating a cute bunny girl from sketch to finish. In the following steps, you'll see how I use a custom Art Brush, Blends, and the Appearance panel in Adobe Illustrator. I'm working in CS5, but the majority of this tutorial can be done in any recent version of the software. While transparent gradients was a CS4 addition, there is a way to get around it if you're creative by creating Blends instead.

1 **Placing the Sketch in Illustrator**

I'll be using a scanned sketch as a base for my illustration. So first I File > Place the sketch on the Artboard, and scale the sketch to fit nicely within the Artboard with the Free Transform Tool (E). Then I set the Opacity of the sketch to 50% and lock the layer. I prefer to keep the sketch layer on top when I trace, so I create new layers beneath the sketch layer.

2 **Tracing the Outline**

I start by tracing the outline with the Pen Tool (P). Set Fill to white and use a black 0.25 pt stroke. I prefer creating different shapes and keeping them separate on their own layers when I am tracing. I start from back to front, so my layers will automatically be the right order from bottom to top. To keep all the layers organized and easy to find, you can label them with descriptive names, such as body, hair, eyes, etc.

❸ Drawing the Eyeballs

I draw the eyeballs using the Ellipse Tool (L). The eyeball I draw may very likely go over the eyelid. Duplicate the eye whites layer, move it above the eyeball layer, and make a Clipping Mask (Ctrl+7). That's a convenient way to move the eyeballs freely and within boundaries.

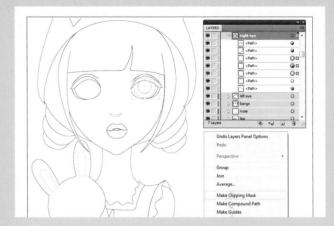

❹ Making an Eyelash Brush

For eyelashes, we will create a custom brush. Draw a triangle shape as shown with a black fill, and add it to the brush panel as a New Art Brush. Under Art Brush Options, set Colorization Method to Tints. This setting will allow you to change the stroke color as you wish. Use the Pen Tool (P) to draw a few curved lines, and apply the brush we just created. Adjust the weight of the stroke to get the result you want.

❺ Adding Solid Colors

Now let's fill in all the shapes with some solid colors. I always start coloring from skin, to hair, then details on face, and clothes. I would like to add a little gothic look in this piece, so I decide to go with pale skin, dark hair, and a muted tone.

6 Detailing the Face

After the base colors are selected, I start adding details and shading. Select the face layer and go to Appearance panel. Add a new fill with a gray radial gradient with 0% Opacity in the center. Do the same for the neck. We will add some blush to her face and shoulder using a pink gradient. Add some white gradients as highlights to her cheekbone.

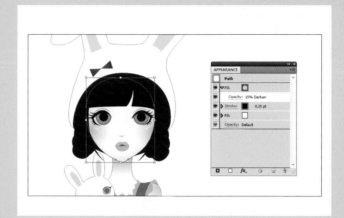

7 Shading the Eyes

For eyes, first we add shading to create the eye socket. Use the Ellipse Tool (L) to create a circle in position of the eye socket and fill it with a gray radial gradient transparent on the edge. Create another circle on top that's slightly smaller with a red gradient. Use the Pen Tool (P) to draw the eyelid and fill it with a gradient that matches the skin color.

8 Finishing the Eyes

Fill the pupil with a linear gradient. Add a shadow along the edge of the eyeball, and add highlights with different transparency to create depth. Use the Pen Tool (P) to draw a new moon shape filled with a dark red gradient behind the eye and on top of the eyelid to soften the hard edge.

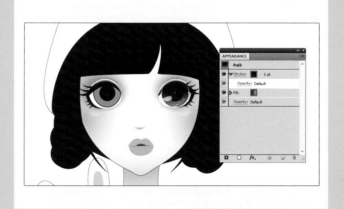

⑨ Filling in the Lips

For the lips, fill with a pink gradient and add shine by creating white dots of different sizes and transparency. Add a few freckles over her nose bridge between the eyes.

⑩ Touching Up the Hair

For the shine effects on her hair, use the Pen Tool (P) to create some zigzag shapes and fill with a gradient that is lighter than the hair. Repeat this process and create some smaller shapes with even lighter colors as the highlight. Add some darker gradients for the shading in her bangs.

⑪ Detailing the Hat

Now let's work on her bunny hat. Open the Appearance panel and add fill with a slightly darker gradient. For the beads, use the Ellipse Tool (L) to draw a circle and fill with a gray radial gradient. Duplicate the bead and place them on both ends. Make a Blend (Ctrl+Alt+B) and modify it to be on a desired curved path.

⓬ Styling the Clothes

For her clothes, add a red gradient using the Appearance panel. For the ruffles, we will use a red gradient fill with transparency for the soft look. Use the Pen Tool (P) to create some folds on the ruffle and fill with darker shade. Fill the glove with a dark color similar to her hair and add some shades.

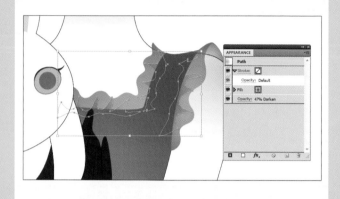

⓭ Adding Details to the Bunny

To add shading and details to the bunny, just repeat the process you applied to the girl. You can add shading, blush, and highlights to the bunny the same way. Now the center image is done!

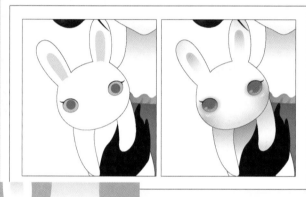

⑭ Framing the Center Image

Next we will frame it up. Use the Ellipse Tool (L) to create an oval, and fill with a gray gradient. You can also add some patterns to give it a textured look. Create another oval on top, 20pt stroke, with no fill. Object > Expand the stroke, select the bottom three anchor points, and move them down 10 pixels. Use a dark gray gradient for the frame and apply Effect > Stylize > Inner Glow to give it depth.

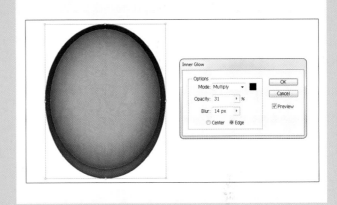

⑮ Decorating the Frame

The frame can use a little extra decoration, so I decide to add some flowers to it. Use the Pen Tool (P) to draw a flower and fill with a light gray gradient. Make two duplicates of the flower and arrange them at the bottom of the frame. The flower shape makes a good pattern for the frame. Make multiple copies of the flower, and create a Clipping Mask (Ctrl+7) using the frame. Change the Blending Mode of the flower pattern layer to Overlay.

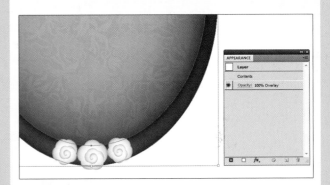

16 Creating the Background

Finally, we will create a background to complete this piece. Use the Rectangle Tool (M) to create the wall using a gray gradient. Create the stripes by making a Blend (Ctrl+Alt+B) of two identical tall rectangles. Set the Blending Mode of the stripes to Multiply with 40% Opacity.

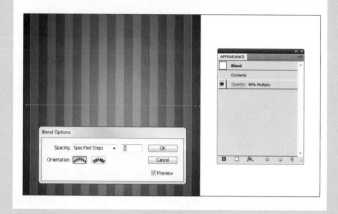

Conclusion

And here's the resulting image!

Adobe Illustrator is a very powerful tool for illustration and is my favorite software. The tools and effects discussed in this tutorial are not too difficult or complex to learn, and when you apply them creatively, you can create a very polished-looking vector artwork with depth and details. I hope you've enjoyed this tutorial on creating a cute bunny girl from sketch to finish!

Rian Saputra

"Engaging the viewer and communicating a message is the main mission for me."

When creating artwork, I have to consider myself a beginner, a little child who's still learning. That way I'll feel no boundaries. I can experiment and play with colors, and the expression of emotions flows smoothly, and the result is often whimsical and affectionate. Role playing is also part of my ritual when making artwork; I think of myself as the subject of the piece so I can study the emotional aspects that need to be expressed visually through familiar signals and gestures. Engaging the viewer and communicating a message is the main mission for me. That's why while I use familiar and representative gesticulation in my artwork.

The first artists who inspired me came from the stories that my family told me when I was a kid. The work of those artists is what my family wanted me to recognize as successful, entertaining fine art. I eagerly doodled on every piece of paper there was, and I sold my very first artwork when I was just eight years old. Mind you, that first illustration was just a bunch of colorful ninjas—not really representing the inspiration that came from those fine artists of the Renaissance period, ironically.

As I grew up, I found more artists to idolize and be inspired by, and along with my artist friends, I became significantly absorbed in vector art and the art industry. These friends helped me grow with their help and friendly competition, and they motivated me in my artwork.

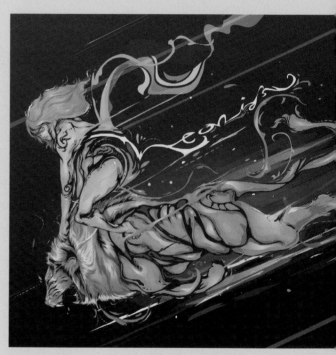

Leonids, 2010

▶ Friendly Kill, 2009

THE END OF DAEVAS

END OF DAEVAS, 2010

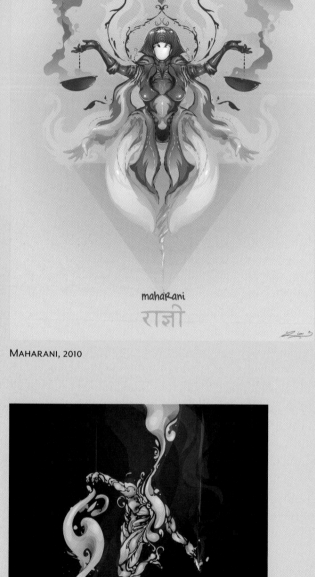

maharani
राज्ञी

MAHARANI, 2010

BARTHOLEMEW, 2009

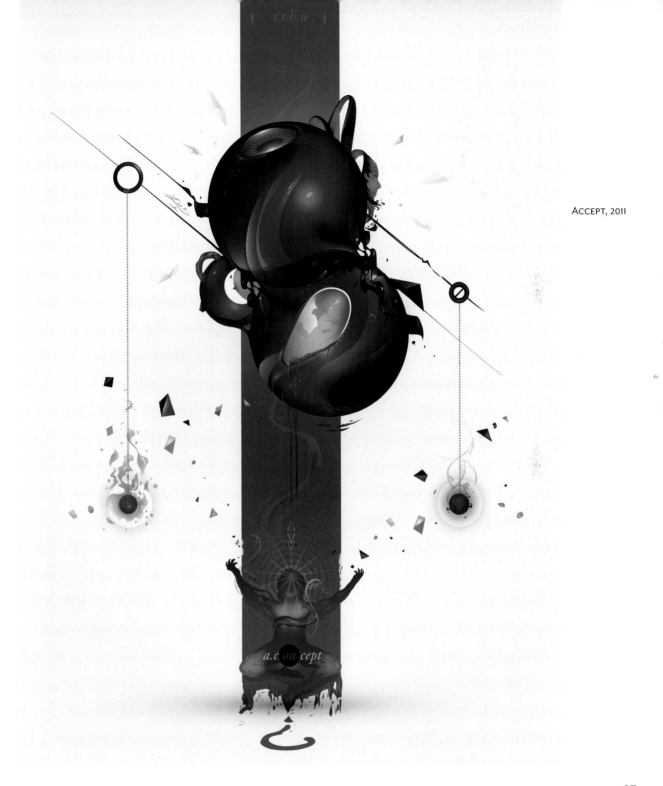

ACCEPT, 2011

Rafael Aguilar Guzmán

I live drawing and painting everything in my mind.

Illustration and animation are my means of expression, while also my work and my life. I am a lover of detail in my work and the multiple readings that I can get into it. I'm always seeking to participate in projects that challenge me and offer me the opportunity to bring something new to the medium in which I work.

I am an animator, illustrator, and designer in México City. My work is inspired by science fiction, fantasy, music, and folklore surreal that exists in Mexico and Asia. I am currently developing my own illustration and animation studio, where I plan to develop all my personal projects that I keep in my sketchbooks.

"I am a lover of detail in my work and the multiple readings that I can get into it."

SERGE THE DANCER, 2011

DISHARMONY CHORDS, 2010

MATTER OF TIME, 2012

ChinKong, 2010

MotherTree, 2011

Chuchin, 2011

Maria Goubar

"I've never
thought of
vector art as
limiting in
any way."

I've been drawing since early childhood. My first inspiration was my mother, who does oil painting. She always supported me and pushed me to draw. Seeing my mother's vividly colored works since childhood made me accustomed to the idea that colors should be bright and energetic and should draw the eye in. She also taught me that it is a lot easier to impart negativity into a painting than to try to have the piece elicit a positive emotional response.

Our house was always filled with art books of fascinating painters and graphic artists. I think it is very important to have books like that around so kids learn at an early age how interesting art can be. Some of my favorite sources of inspiration were books with the works of Dutch painter Hierony-mus Bosch and graphic artists Aubrey Beardsley and Alphonse Mucha, as well as a black-and-white edition of the Old Testament with amazing etchings by Julius Schnorr von Carolsfeld. These days I am inspired a lot by artists, movies, TV shows, and animation. Often when you see something that captures your imagination you want to draw more and create, so that one day you can be the one who captures other people's imagination.

For a long time I did only graphics (quills, ink, and paper) and thought of myself as simply a graphic artist. Then I received a gift of a Wacom tablet and a laptop, and my curiosity toward the new format led me to experiment. I've never thought of vector art as limiting in any way. In essence, it's the same as using oil on a canvas, with strokes and colored objects put together. This is what I'd try to remember when something wasn't working out. I believe that the difference between raster and vector is mostly in our heads, and that often results in over-simplifying and making it much less detailed and with fewer colors than in raster art.

Dream Again, 2009

▶ Sailor Saturn, 2011

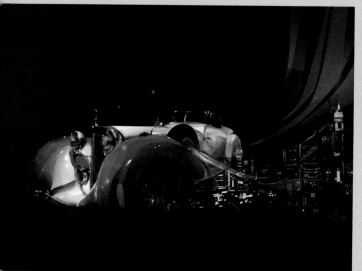

SUMMIT OF ONE'S DESIRES, 2006

LAKESIDE, 2007

◀ CAKE, 2011

PIRATE, 2006

Using Opacities in a Creative Illustration

In this tutorial you'll learn how to create an illustration of a character drawing a hand—which is also drawing her—in Adobe Illustrator. I'll show you the benefits of using gradients, blurs, and a variety of blending modes and opacities.

1 **Creating the Sketch**

First create the drawing with the Pencil Tool (N). Group (Ctrl+G) the drawing and place it on a separate layer, making the layer's Opacity setting lower than the one before it.

The group is set to Blending Mode Multiply. Later on, when you'll be working with color, this mode will let the drawing softly overlay the color.

2 **Adding Color and Blurs**

Don't be afraid to go beyond the edges of the drawing. The lack of borders is what will give your drawing its picturesque quality. And don't limit yourself; enjoy the color. In Illustrator there is an effect called Gaussian Blur that softens the edges of an object. The downside is that you can see the pixels when you zoom in. Use this effect only in the beginning, drawing over it to conceal the pixels afterward.

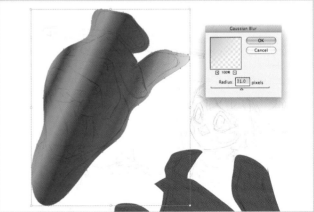

❸ Using Gradients for Shadows

Transparent radial gradients can be used in place of blurs. Here, using this gradient you can roughly mark out the shadows on the wings of the character.

❹ Applying the Chalk Art Brush

Using the same gradient and changing colors, highlight the hair, lighting the edges with blue. To convey the idea behind the drawing—that the character and the hand are drawing each other—pick one of the default Illustrator Art Brushes called Chalk. Change the brush size to large and create an organic-looking, uneven edge.

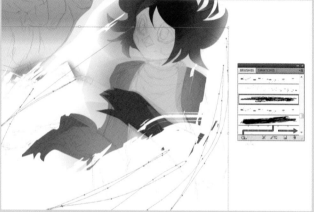

❺ Applying the Color Burn Blending Mode

I really like the Color Burn blending mode. It can often yield unexpected color combinations. This will make the piece more vivid and you'll be able to move past the color combinations that you have gotten accustomed to. However, use Color Burn with caution. If you use it too crudely and in excess, the colors will quickly become unappealing and result in too much contrast.

6 **Hiding Overlapping Edges**

Don't be afraid to go beyond the edges of your drawing; you can always cover anything extra with the background color. Choosing light colors and using a gradient, light the character's face and put shadows on the hand.

7 **Applying Gradients to Soften**

Next, work on achieving smooth transitions from one color to another. It is important for the gradient to soften the transition from the color to transparency, not from one color to another. Otherwise when you layer one object on top of another, the object's edges will show.

8 **Enhancing the Lighting**

Now you can work on the lighting in more detail. I'll show you a convenient trick: hatching with objects with very low opacity. Drawing many such objects, one on top of the other, you can create an illusion of a gradual transition from one color to another. In this screen shot smooth transitions on the farthest cheek and the shadow from the nose are achieved using many tens of such almost transparent objects. Using this method, you can easily add a tint, a soft but not too washed-out reflection of light.

⑨ Creating a New Calligraphic Brush

A line should look alive. It looks dull when you create a contour with a single width. To liven up a line, create several brushes with pressure sensitivity. Then use them to work on the small details, adding decorative elements to the illustration.

⑩ Applying Line Art

Using the same brushes you created in the previous step, detail the edge of the hair and eyes. Using the background color, go over the contours thoroughly. In traditional drawing, the eraser doesn't only have to have a minor helping part but can also be a full-fledged drawing tool. Here you are employing the same principle to remove unneeded elements using the background color and making the outline varied and interesting.

⑪ Modifying Shapes with the Eraser Tool

The Eraser (Shift+E) is another convenient tool. Make it pressure sensitive. Unlike with the Knife Tool, using the Eraser on gradients will not shift the colors. You can use it to cut good-looking shapes out of the gradients.

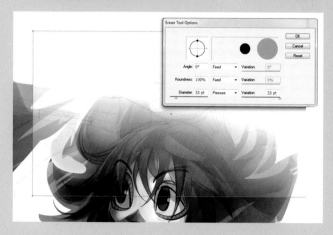

⑫ Adding Atmosphere to the Hair

Using a gradient, create the illusion that the hair is gradually dissolving in a white haze. Then, use the Eraser Tool (Shift+E) to bring back the saturated color so it looks like it's flowing down the character's head.

⑬ Hiding the Sketch

During the drawing process you can remove parts of the sketch that are already unnecessary so they don't cause a distraction and so you can see the illustration as a whole. Now and then turn off the layer with the sketch and look at the illustration without it. Without the sketch visible, you can add more subtle color transitions and accents.

⑭ Adding Light and Shadow

You can create large objects that fall over several surfaces at once. This way, you're providing a wholeness to the illustration. Use blending modes to enhance the contrast of light and shadow.

⑮ Using Blending Mode Color Dodge

When adding light to your drawing, if it has a white background or a large white area, you can set your Blending Mode to Color Dodge. Any overlapping of the object with this Blending Mode will not affect the white, as it becomes invisible. You can draw a large object and unite several parts of the image. Doing so will not cause extra fragmentation.

⑯ Using Colorful Gradients

Color Dodge can give an interesting effect when you lay a two-color gradient onto half-transparent objects that don't have a background. This way, you can use one object to draw both light and shadows.

⑰ Adding Brush Details

When you want to draw brightly shining metal, draw a light blue/gray object. Blue/gray is used for shadows and shading, and light blue for light. Then, in Color Dodge blending mode, you draw a gleam in bright orange. The gleam looks warm and gives the object a realistic look.

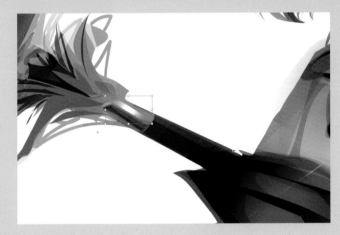

⑱ Modifying Object Opacities

With the end in sight, zoom in closely to work on the small details. Try to avoid using objects in Normal 100%. Otherwise the drawing will lose its picturesque quality. Even if you need to use a bright color, use, let's say 86%–90%, so the lower layers show a bit through the color.

⑲ Keeping a Consistent Style

Using the hatching with highly transparent objects of different colors (see Step 8), you can start to work on the hand. I use hatching like this when I draw portraits or human body parts. This way, you can quickly give an object dimension and avoid sharp vector edges that distract from the form. To bring the image together, draw abstract shapes in the background. When drawing them, try to align the shapes with the movement of the characters.

20 Adding Highlights

Highlights and bright reflections of light draw the eye in—this is all worth doing in the end. You shouldn't start on them before you work on the shading, light, and shadows. Highlights can easily fragment an illustration. For light reflections, use the Hard Light blending mode.

21 Creating Finer Details

With Blending Mode Multiply it's easy to draw faint, small decorative elements; patterns on fabric; or as in this case, a pattern of feathers on the character's wings.

㉒ Refining the Wings

You've reached the last stage: detailing of the wings. I left them for the end because you can see the illustration marked out in tone and color, as a whole. There is no need to draw the wings out until this point. Now they won't be obscured by objects from other parts of the drawing, and the tips of the wings look sharp and contrasting. When everything is done, remove the layer with the drawing and group all the objects. Then apply Object/Expand Appearance to the group. You can easily transform the size of the image, making it larger or smaller on the page.

Conclusion

I use these basic concepts of highlighting, shadows, blurs, and gradients in the majority of my artwork. They help create a soft edge with plenty of detailing. This illustration would look great in an editorial setting or as an illustration in a children's book.

Ekaterina Dedova

"It's not a casual choice. I'm mesmerized by (vector graphics') elegance and pureness."

I am a freelance illustrator, specializing in vector graphics. It's not a casual choice. I'm mesmerized by its elegance and pureness. At the beginning of my career I was passionately fond of pinup art and French vector artists like Arthur de Pins and Lillycat.

As the years went by and my style was maturing, I began to admire the concept and character artists for their fantastic way to paint lights and color. At this point the vector graphics became some kind of challenge for me. Trying to elude its limitations, I began to experiment with various instruments and techniques: patterns, special effects, and Live Trace for some vector textures. In this way I could find my own way to draw, making my illustrations more expressive.

I'm still loving pinup girls and 50s, but I want to tell stories. Ambiguous and incomplete stories that leave space for the imagination of my spectators.

Carnival Time, 2011

EMO PUPPY, 2011

HANAMI 1, 2010

HANAMI 3, 2011

ELEGANCE OF BLACK AND WHITE, 2010

AUTUMN STORIES, 2010

Cindel Ribbens

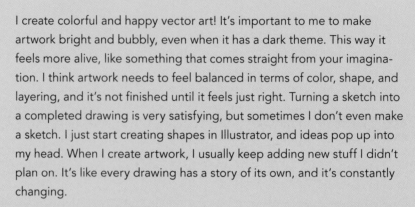

"That's what making art is all about, letting your imagination loose!"

I create colorful and happy vector art! It's important to me to make artwork bright and bubbly, even when it has a dark theme. This way it feels more alive, like something that comes straight from your imagination. I think artwork needs to feel balanced in terms of color, shape, and layering, and it's not finished until it feels just right. Turning a sketch into a completed drawing is very satisfying, but sometimes I don't even make a sketch. I just start creating shapes in Illustrator, and ideas pop up into my head. When I create artwork, I usually keep adding new stuff I didn't plan on. It's like every drawing has a story of its own, and it's constantly changing.

I used Photoshop when I was studying media design, and that's how I discovered Illustrator. It fascinated me. I really liked the smooth shapes I could make with it. I wanted to learn how to make vector art to make the quirky and strange things from my imagination more real—mixing animals with monsters, candy, and fruits, and making it all look slightly off. I created a very colorful world of my own.

I never took Illustrator classes; I learned just by experimenting and am completely self-taught. My favorite tools are the Pen Tool and Gradient Tool. I like to add as many colors as possible to an artwork to create depth. Vector art can look really flat. I don't want my work to look bland, so I layer a lot to give everything more shape and depth. I love experimenting with colors by layering gradients to see what happens. I use the color sliders a lot when I work; this way it's easier to see what works together and what doesn't. I never decide beforehand what color I want a certain object to have; I just choose the color that feels right at that moment. That's what making art is all about, letting your imagination loose!

PARADISE, 2010

▶ INTERSTELLAR FRIENDS, 2010

HAU'OLI, 2011

MAD TEA PARTY, 2011

KOINOBORI, 2011

ARCTIC UNICORNS, 2011

Aedel Fakhrie

"I am still developing what I call a *vector painting* technique."

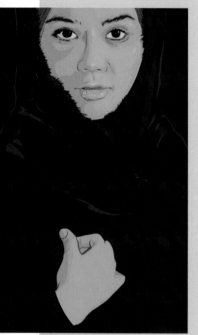

BELOVED ONE, 2011

Movies, music, and games are the main sources of inspiration and imagination for my artwork. Sometimes I combine all those things with actual occurrences in this world. I've studied great artists from the past and now, and each of them has different stories and styles. I learn from them what is the point and the concept of making some cool and great artwork. I've used all these references to help me build my own style and characteristic. I also learn from my old works and upgrade the technique and quality.

My favorite tools in Adobe Illustrator are the Pencil Tool and the Pen Tool, which allow me to make a lot of vector objects into abstract, surreal, or realistic shapes and styles. I am still developing what I call a *vector painting* technique.

I work as digital artist at VOXLAB in Singapore. I am an illustrator, and I also do design composition and art direction. I also offer illustration or design consultation to clients or will suggest a fresh idea to the clients without involving my own illustration style. I like to work as part of a team because of the new knowledge and experience I can gain from my teammates. For me, learning something new is fun, and there's no limit on visual creativity. I feel so lucky because I am always thirsty for new ideas, I love to share with others, and I gain more experience from other creative people. Someone once wrote, "Work hard and keep humble." These words are really cool.

RABIES JUNKYARD, 2010

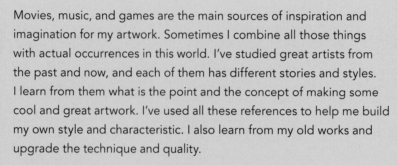

HONEY POISON AND MY COUNTRY, 2012

GIMME FUEL, 2011

The Ocktober, 2011

The Deadly Twin, 2010

Creating a Sports Shoe Illustration from a Sketch

In this tutorial I'll show you how to lend an emotional effect to an object (a shoe) using Adobe Illustrator. Some of the tools you'll be using are the Pen Tool (P) and gradients, along with a graphics tablet.

1 **Creating Base Shapes**

Once you've imported your sketch into Illustrator, use the Pen Tool (P) to trace it, adding a lot of detail to get a better result. In the following image, the red outline marks where the highlights will appear and the black outline where the shapes and details will come in. The dashed line represents the shoe stitching.

2 **Adding Color**

Selecting the black outline, switch it to Fill rather than Stroke. Fill it in with a base color and use a darker shade to make the detailing and darker areas pop.

❸ Adding Shade with Gradients

In this step, use gradients to add more detail and shaded areas to the shoe. Be sure to lower the Opacity setting and set Blending Mode to Multiply.

❹ Refining the Shading

Selecting the red outline, again use a gradient (only this time don't set Blending Mode to Multiply so that the gradient remains bright) to fill it in and remove the red stroke around it.

❺ Adding Subtle Line Art

Next create a new layer called Stroke Brush. Select the brush profile in the Stroke panel, set Stroke Weight to 0.5pt, and using a dark gray color, add more detail to the shoe with the Pen Tool (P) and/or the Pencil Tool (N).

6 **Duplicating the Illustration**

Create a new layer and name it extra-outline. Select
everything and Group it together (Ctrl+G); then
duplicate it into the extra-outline layer.

7 **Changing the Fill to a Stroke**

Select the extra-outline layer and delete the fill
colors. Change the stroke color to magenta and the
Stroke Weight to 0.25pt.

8 **Hiding the Original Shoe**

Remove several paths on the magenta outline to
avoid having it look crowded.

❾ Repositioning the Duplicate

Move the magenta outline back on top of the solid-colored shoe illustration. You can then increase the size of the outline and set Blending Mode to Color Dodge.

❿ Distorting the Lines

Using the Direct Selection Tool (A), stretch and spread several of the magenta-colored outlines as shown here.

⓫ Adding Zigzag Lines

Create a new layer and name it Composition Objects. Lock the other layers. Using the Pen Tool (P), create shapes with a white fill, placing them on top of the shoe in a way that works with the composition.

⑫ **Modifying the Composition**
Keep adding shapes using the Ellipse Tool (L), Text
Tool (T), Pencil Tool (N), and Pen Tool (P). Use the
Pathfinder panel to break some of the shapes apart.
Just keep on adding until you're happy with the
composition and look.

⑬ **A Final Gradient**
Finally, work on the canvas layout, using a gradient
with light tones to complement the shoe and its
shapes.

Conclusion

As you can see, all you need are some simple and easy-to-make objects to
build an impression. As long as you have an idea of the style and the composition you want, it all works out in the end.

Justin Currie

"I feel that I'm chasing my best pieces of artwork—in an annoying and fantastic way."

RAIN, 2011

My background is in traditional illustration, graphic design, and the art of constantly doodling on school papers. Somehow this all culminated in a vector-based illustration style that I couldn't be happier with. My number one goal with all of my art is to invoke a "wow" reaction. My work tends to focus on scenes of sci-fi or fantasy epicness. I love to create pieces that hint at an extensive backstory, letting the viewer's mind race with questions. I also especially enjoy drawing anything with the huge-versus-small size relationship. Oversized robots and gargantuan dragons make regular appearances in my work, alongside tiny counterparts.

I decided to call my style *Shattered Vector Painting*. This name came from the frequent comments along the lines of, "What's this process called? It looks like broken glass." "Well," I'd say, "it's vector, and I use a lot of broken-up pieces." So "shattered vector" became my standard reply. I think my biggest achievement is the development of a recognizable style. Growing up as an aspiring artist, I constantly struggled and pondered over what kind of style I would end up having, spending a lot of my time trying to emulate peer artists' techniques and looks. And then, somewhere along the line, I suddenly had my own look, and it is an amazing thing to have. I realize now your style is just something that needs to organically emerge.

I work under the handle Chasing Artwork. If you're always drawing, you're always improving. So, in a way, I feel that I'm chasing my best pieces of artwork—in an annoying and fantastic way. My best piece is always going to be the next one.

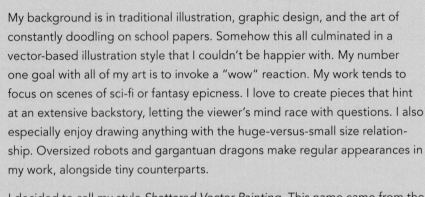

EMPRESS, 2012

COLDFIRE, 2012

INFERNO, 2011

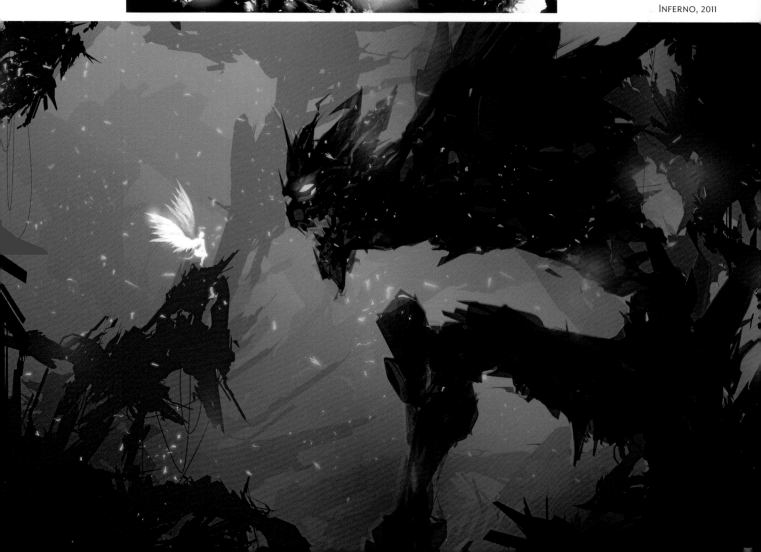

Nastasia Peters

"Designing the characters and their environments is something I love to do."

My drawings are a way for me to communicate the stories that are in my mind. Designing the characters and their environments is something I love to do, and I hope that one day they'll stand out and be recognized.

While my coloring methods vary, the one thing that always remains the same is the line art. Doing the line art in vector gives me more control over the detailing. I developed my own style and know how to work it with barely any thinking.

I am a fantasy illustrator, so most of my drawings are scenes or representations of some form of fantasy element, be it sorcerers, magical creatures, or warriors. They are what I see floating around in my head, and I simply transfer them over onto a digital canvas. Currently, I'm working on illustrations to accompany a novel I wrote. It forces me to work on getting atmospheres right and capturing important moments from written words.

NARA, 2012

RANGERS ALLEY, 2012

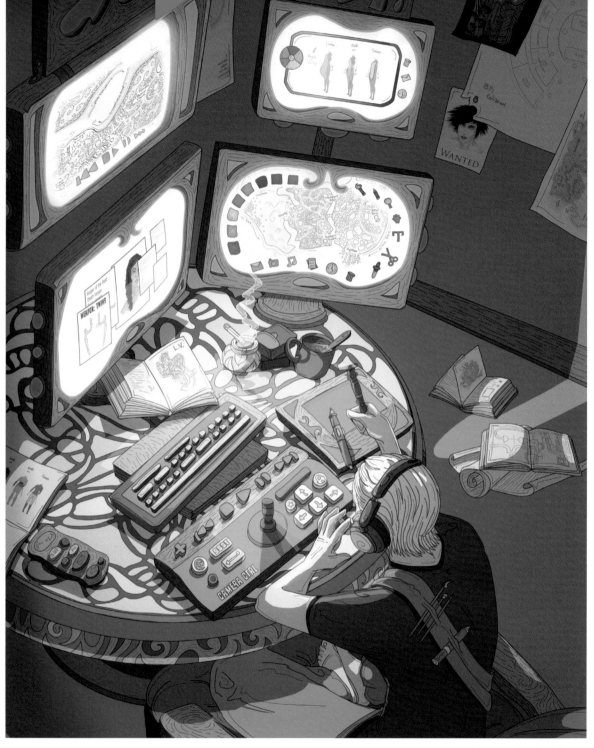

WISE A EXTRAORDINAIRE, 2012

VOODOO AND VAMPIRE DOGS, 2012

PALLIUM CASTLE, 2011

BREAK OF DAWN, 2012

Creating a Colorful Fantasy Trio Using the Pencil Tool

In this tutorial I'll show you how I create my line art using Adobe Illustrator and share an overview of how I put in colors. A few tools and effects I'll be using are the Pencil Tool (N), Live Paint (Shift+L), Blends (W), and my graphics tablet. Most of my drawings are illustrations for stories I've written, and here I've drawn characters in a certain way to illustrate the relationship they share with one another.

1 **Placing the Sketch in Illustrator**

I sketch my drawings in Adobe Photoshop as I'm already using it to cut, glue, and put together my references (personal stock). Once done, I choose File > Place to move the sketch into Adobe Illustrator, lower the Opacity setting of the image to about 50%, and lock it. Then I can begin working on the line art.

2 **Creating the Skeleton Line Art**

I create several folders, and Step 2 focuses on the one titled Skeleton. It shows the first lines I've drawn over the sketch: the general, undetailed shapes of the characters. I use the Pencil Tool (N) to draw these, selecting a dark brown color and setting it on toggle Stroke (X) with a Stroke Weight of 0.6pt rather than toggle Fill (X). I find that when the line art is too thick and too dark, it winds up taking too much focus once the colors are in. For the sword, I use the Pen Tool (P) because it lets me draw straighter lines. For the gold coins I use the Ellipse Tool (L).

3 Adding Detailed Line Art

Using a Stroke Weight of 0.3pt (Layer title: Details), I draw thinner and unconnected lines within the skeleton shape, trying to make the characters less flat. Although I don't know in advance where I will put them, I find them to be most aesthetically pleasing in areas such as folds in clothes or where you'll find joints in the human body.

4 Adding Textured Line Art

Still using the Pencil Tool (N) and a dark brown color on the outline setting, I thin the Stroke Weight further, setting it to 0.2pt and drawing in the folder called Extras. Here I add clothing details, such as the patterns on the scarves, the fishnet shirt on the girl, or the metal arm protection on the soldier. I usually draw them freehand rather than using Illustrator patterns because doing so allows me to follow body curves.

5 Using Filled Shapes for Line Art

For the characters' faces I use toggle Fill (X) rather than Stroke, as I want the facial features to be less uniform and vary in thickness, which I can't do with a toggle Stroke (X) set to a certain Stroke Weight. I also outline the background in this step with the Ellipse Tool (L) along with the Line Segment Tool (\) to create the three sections inside the circle. The Stroke Weight of the outline/line art of the background is at 0.8pt. Using the Scissors Tool (C), I remove the lines of the background that overlap the characters.

6 **Adding Color with Live Paint**

Putting all the line art in one layer, I duplicate it, set the original on Blending Mode Multiply, and lock it. Next I go to the copy, which I then title LP, for Live Paint (Shift+L). After filling the line art using the Live Paint Bucket (K), I remove the line art and toggle the fill of the facial features. Then I start putting in the colors. To make it easier on the eyes, I press Ctrl+H so that the lines become invisible but remain selected.

7 **Using the Transparency Panel**

To make the colors a bit less flat, I copy the LP layer and call that layer GR. Then select it and put in a Gradient (>). I set it to Blending Mode Overlay, lowering its Opacity setting somewhere between 20% and 30%. When I want a darker atmosphere, I set the gradient layer to Blending Mode Multiply. I tone down the base colors (layer LP) in Opacity as well to 80%, duplicating that layer (layer White), setting it back to a 100% Opacity, and filling it with white. That way, I make sure the base colors don't turn out to be transparent once I start on the background.

8 **Adding Depth with Shadows**

Again using the Pencil Tool (N), I create a folder titled Shades, select a dark brown, and begin drawing the shadow shapes in toggle Fill (X). Next I select the layer, set it to Blending Mode Multiply, and lower the Opacity. Since I'm still going for a soft atmosphere, I keep my shadows below 50% Opacity.

⑨ Adjusting the Composition

I don't always stick to the initial idea I had to begin with, so I remove the three sections I'd made in the circle—I now want to create a ceiling window instead so its shadow can land on top of the characters. I use the Paintbrush Tool (B) set to toggle Stroke (X) to quickly sketch out the shape of the window's shadow (as shown beneath the layer window). Then using a dark yellow, I begin shaping it out with both the Pen Tool (P) and Pencil Tool (N). I set it to Blending Mode Multiply and lower its Opacity to 30%.

⑩ Rendering the Clouds

I sometimes draw random landscapes, which I later end up using in one of my more elaborate drawings. Such was the case here. In this cloudscape, I use the Pencil Tool (N), toggle Fill (X), and begin shaping the clouds. I start with the darker areas, using new layers with darker tones to place on top of each other until I decide I have enough shapes.

⑪ Adding Cloud Detailing

For the highlights I use several Art Brushes with the Paintbrush Tool (B) to place on top of the darker areas, lowering their Opacity so that they blend in with the darker tones and to make the clouds fluffier and shinier. I create a New Art Brush from two circles (L) and make them into a Blend (Ctrl+Alt+B). Setting my Art Brush to toggle Stroke (X), I vary the Stroke Weight between 0.5pt and 1pt and draw softer edges in the clouds.

⑫ **Rendering the Landscape**
I draw the grass the same way I did the clouds. I had separated the grass from the clouds in different folders—that way, I didn't need to dissect them to be able to use them the way I wanted beneath my characters in the circular platform.

⑬ **Incorporating the Landscape into the Composition**
I turn the grass and clouds into Symbols and place them into the composition where the characters are using the Symbol Sprayer Tool (Shift+S).

⑭ **Adding Detail with a Blend Art Brush**
Remembering I drew gold in this image, I use a soft yellow to create a circular Blend (Ctrl+Alt+ B), turn it into an Art Brush, and set it to toggle Stroke (X). I then use a 0.2pt Stroke Weight to draw quick soft lines on the parts that need to become shiny. Once that's done, I set the layer (named Shines) to Blending Mode Screen and lower its Opacity to 50%.

Conclusion

Lastly, I modify the orientation and draw in additional detailing using the Pencil Tool to ensure there aren't any unnecessary spaces, and it's done! This illustration can accompany text in book form or be used as a poster on a wall. Because the focal point takes place in the center of the image, you can flip it in any direction, viewing it as a portrait or landscape. This art makes a pretty neat wallpaper too!

Charlene Chua

"My approach towards my craft was pieced together from my own experiences in work and life."

◀ Sun Hat, 2012

I consider myself to be a problem solver and an artist. As an illustrator, I feel it is my job to aesthetically address the needs of every brief I am presented; it is never about sitting around to create a picture that satisfies my own creative need.

I started my creative career by getting a job doing cartoon illustrations at a company that created training CD-ROMs. Eventually, I pursued other design and creative management positions. I never had the opportunity to study illustration; my approach towards my craft was pieced together from my own experiences in work and life. I believe these experiences all contribute to affect the artwork.

My style has changed since I started doing illustration in Singapore in 2004. It has been variously described as *manga*, *cartoon*, *colorful*, *Asian*. I think the work has changed a lot since I moved to Canada, and in the last couple of years it has evolved into something more realistic in style and content.

I hope that my artwork continues to serve its purpose throughout the rest of my career. I enjoy making pictures that people find attractive, but I also enjoy helping clients to create unique solutions. I do hope to continue to explore and discover my artistic side and find new techniques that will help keep my work fresh for years to come.

DRAGON FLOWER, 2010

Skaters, 2010

Rockstar, 2008

Ashley S. Benson

"I am a freelance vector artist with a love of all things potently colorful."

I am a freelance vector artist with a love of all things potently colorful. My program of choice has always been and will forever be Adobe Illustrator. When I was introduced to the world of vector, I had no clue how much this complex mathematical program would change and enrich my life.

I was a person who was very afraid of color and mistakes. I worked lightly and hated the idea of permanence. With Adobe Illustrator, I have come out of my shell and brightened my drab and dreary world with explosive color and experimentation.

In my college years, we had a difficult love-hate romance, but as both of us matured and took the time to really get to know each other, we found ourselves not only compatible but also inseparable. We celebrated our six-year anniversary last May, and I'm happy to say the children all resemble Adobe Illustrator, especially in the eyes and nose. I was also very fortunate to have a mother and grandmother who fully supported us.

Malice and Her Friends, 2010

PRINCESS MAYIL AND
THE PEACOCK, 2012

2012

THE WINTER WITCH, 2012

LA BELLEZA DE LA MUERTE, 2011

MOTHER MADE HER, 2011

From Sketch to Finish, *Royal Jelly*

Royal Jelly is a sketch I created with the intention of showing you how to use a handful of Adobe Illustrator tools and effects, including the Gradient Tool, Transparencies, Gaussian Blur Effect, and the Paintbrush Tool. I'll also demonstrate how easy it is to use a sketch or stock but maintain your flexibility. Unforeseen changes can arise, and being able to keep an open mind can expose your project to a world of better options.

❶ Placing the Sketch

My original sketch may look completely set, but this is all subject to change as well. My main focus is the female pose and certain key insects and their placement. I use File > Place to place my sketch on the Artboard.

❷ Creating Skin Base Shapes

Here I focus on the shape of the body using my old friend the Pen Tool (P) as well as Gradients (G) to carve out the basic shapes. I use a Light Umber with Reddish hues for my darker tone, and a Blushed Beige for my lighter tones, working in a Linear Gradient (which I run at an angle to support my light source direction). I have a window in the background of the sketch so that the light will cover more of my character's face than her body.

❸ Using Gradients to Add Detail

I'm using the Gradient Tool (G) once again at an opacity of 46%, but here I'm making good use of my radial gradient selection. I'm using my light peach to transparent option. Transparent gradients are a feature you'll find in Illustrator CS5 and later, but this is just the lazy way to do it. All Adobe Illustrator programs have some sort of gradient available, so the blending of your colors is all in the effort of tweaking to get a seamless coverage.

❹ Drawing Wings from Stock

On a new layer, following along the vein pathways of the wing with my Pen Tool (P), I change my settings to a Stroke Weight of 1pt and create various line segments until I've completed the wing. From there, I'll choose Select All and from the top toolbar choose Options > Expand, leaving both the Fill and Stroke options selected. This enables me to treat my stroke line as a fill. I can now use gradients with it, and if I'm comfortable with where my lines are, I can combine all the segments by using Pathfinder (Shift+Ctrl+F9) and the Unite option.

❺ Creating a Soft, Flowing Dress

I use a number of gradients in dark brown to reddish-brown tones layered in opacities averaging between 20% and 72% on this dress. Using a reddish-orange I include a few highlights by using the Feather Effect with a feather radius of 0.13in. I group all the pieces together and make a duplicate layer, dropping the Opacity to 28% and adding a Gaussian Blur Effect with a radius of 4.7 pixels.

6 **Beginning the Hair**

Here, I'm using dark brown tones to light brown tones in a linear gradient. I've kept my main layer at a diminished opacity so that I can still see the hairline of my sketch.

7 **Adding Strand Detailing to the Hair**

I take my finished hair and group it (Ctrl+G) into a manageable bundle. I then duplicate this layer and, using a Gaussian Blur of 2.8 pixels and an opacity setting of 29%, give my character's hair an almost effortless softness.

8 **Creating a Flowing Scarf**

I'm adding the scarf details in the same manner as the dress, so think of this step as a repetition of how the dress fabric is handled. I also provide greater detail with gold trim and gold bracelets. I create the honeycomb effect by overlaying shapes made by the Polygon Tool onto a single layer. After grouping these polygon shapes together (by selecting them and pressing Ctrl+G), I select the bracelet shape as well by pressing Alt+Shift. I revisit Pathfinder (Shift+Ctrl+F9) and select the Minus Front feature to cut out my Polygon shapes.

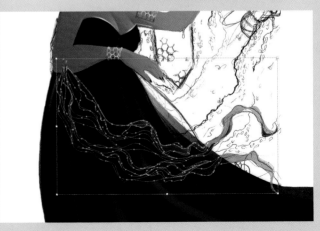

⑨ Altering the Composition Dimensions

I decide that I want to make my overall composition larger. I revisit my Document Setup and change my presets to reflect an additional 6". This gives me a perfect square at 17"x17". I make my projects bigger than necessary just in case I'll need a larger size later on. As it stands, I can later shrink to a more manageable size after I finish.

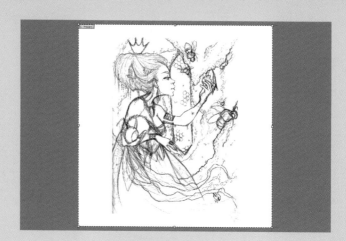

⑩ Resizing the Illustration

I've selected all of my layers and enlarged the project. When you do this, don't forget to enlarge your sketch, which tends to be an easy thing to forget. I found that in doing this, I was still off by a few inches toward the ends of the dress. Using the Direct Selection Tool (A) over the area in question and dragging from the ends, you can manipulate the grouped shapes and extend them; later on you can make any corrections to any ill-mannered curves by again using the Direct Selection Tool (A) and grabbing the handles to readjust them.

⑪ Beginning in the Background

In this step I start adding the background. My layers are in a radial gradient and run from a burnt orange to a deep brown umber color. My Pen Tool (P) work is textured to give the appearance of a natural honeycombed environment. Nothing is perfect in nature because it's the flaws that make it all wonderful.

⑫ Adding a Soft Glow

I'm overlaying another gradient, but with brighter hues. Using a tangerine yellow to burnt orange gradient and then overlaying a Feathered Effect (Effect > Style > Feather) at a radius of 0.25 inches, I have an instant glow that gives the appearance of light bouncing off the honeycomb from the open window. Depending on how much light I want to perceive this window is giving off, I can adjust the opacity setting of my layer.

⑬ Balancing Brightness

I notice there's a little too much brightness to my female form. It's lacking depth and looks too flat. To address this problem, I make a rough layer of her form in a dark brown and overlay a Feathered Effect (Effect > Style > Feather) at a radius of 0.63 inches and an opacity value of 19%. I use my Eraser Tool (Shift+E) to cut out the form of her dragonfly ornament, because I want to omit more light in that area.

⑭ Refining the Hair

Though I love how my character's hair came out, I aim for that little extra effort that makes things worthwhile. Using the Gradient Tool (G) yet again, I take a bright white to Invisible in a Radial pattern and make small facets of light that give the hair depth. Remember, if you don't have a version of Illustrator that allows Color to Invisible, it's just a matter of using a similar color to substitute for the Invisible option.

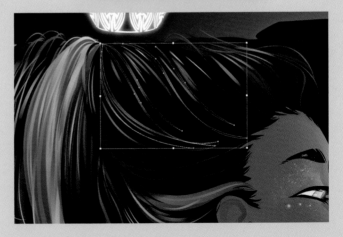

⑮ Working on the Honeycomb

In this step, I begin to form the texture of the honey-comb using the Eclipse Tool (L) and Gradient Tool (G) using the same coloring as the honeycomb shapes. I turn the opacity to 19% to blend the surface to the base.

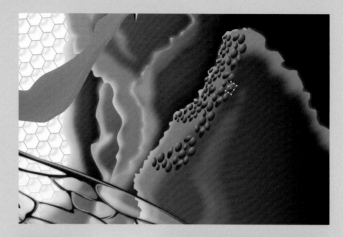

⑯ Adding Glowing Honey

The honey is made from a combination of Gradients ranging from light cream, to golden yellow, to burnt orange using the radial gradient option and an opacity setting of 76%. Next, I group all these layers together, duplicate the grouping, and use a Gaussian Blur with a radius of 1.8 pixels and an opacity of 19% to make the honey glow.

⑰ Adding the Foreground Details

All the honey is finished and a layer of pollen is added to the foreground. I make the pollen by using the Gaussian Blur Effect and a setting of 4.1 pixels.

⑱ Using Stock as a Reference to Create a Bee

Here I've started working on what I like to call the Big Baby Bee. My initial vector work is made with only radial gradients ranging from honey yellow to dark brown umber fill. The eyes are made with a gradient of light purple to dark purple at an opacity of 51%. I added a solid black layer underneath to give it the diffused coloring you see now.

⑲ Adding Fur to the Bee

The bee's fur is made using the Paintbrush Tool (B) and a tapered Art Brush. Once I finish my bee hairs, I do a grouping (Ctrl+G) and duplicate the set. I use a Gaussian Blur Effect of 2.8 pixels and an opacity of 60%.

⑳ Saving the Bees for Future Projects

I decide to duplicate the bee and make it into a symbol that can be multiplied but that will help to reduce my file size. I select the bee and choose Window > Symbols (Shift+Ctrl+F11) and then the New Symbol option. The bee should now appear as a Symbol Icon in the Symbol window.

Conclusion

By the end of this project, we have a completed a fun and fancy piece, ready for printing. Having a program with such flexibility is what led me to fall in love with Adobe Illustrator. It helps to have a forgiving medium, and with each new version that comes out, the possibilities for improvement get bigger and better!

Grelin Machin

"My art universe is a carnival filled with candy, sexual innuendo, and monsters."

The first time I worked with Illustrator in my design class, I swore I was never going to touch it again. Shortly thereafter, I discovered vector art and fell in love with it.

My art universe is a carnival filled with candy, sexual innuendo, and monsters; anything can happen there. My creatures are ready to eat or kill each other to get the attention of the girl or to protect her from other characters. Sometimes they are making plots together; we never know for sure with them! Most of my artwork is a combination of death drive and life instinct.

I consider myself a varied artist: I paint on wood panels and make plushies and sculptures. I need to be versatile to keep being inspired, but I make most of my work with vector. It's the only media satisfying my obsession for perfect curves and gradients. I studied design graphic for many years, but two years ago I made the choice to become an artist instead of graphic designer. I took the risk and chose a more uncertain road, but now I'm happier than ever.

Ten years ago, a teacher told me that vector art would never have the warmth of a traditional painting. Nowadays, I think I, and many other artists, proved him wrong.

THE IMPOSSIBLE LOVE OF A GENTLEWORM, 2012

SAMANTHA AND
THE ANATOMY OF
HALLOWEEN, 2011

SHE BELONGS TO US NOW, 2012

SAUSAGE SORCERESS WITH MINION, 2012

SWALLOW THE LEADER, 2011

GENTLEMEN DRINKING TEA, 2012

Maria Dimova

Adobe Illustrator was the first graphic program I was introduced to. I fell in love with it right away and it became the only program I work with. Brushes are my favorite Adobe Illustrator tool. Usually I create my own brushes and draw all the contours with it. My favorite color combinations are: orange and turquoise; blue and the color of ripe cherries; and almost all works of mine contain gold and silver colors.

One of the main motives of my art is feminine beauty, which I like to shade in splendid clothes with complicated ornaments and rich refinement.

Of course, I'm inspired by the great masters who created in the Renaissance epoch, but mostly I'm influenced by the Pre-Raphaelites and Modern graphic arts. I'm very interested in the fantasy genre—in graphic arts as well as in literature. That's why I try to add at least a bit of magic in my works.

Usually my creative process includes several stages: idea, reference search, a pencil sketch, a plane brush drawing in Adobe Illustrator, and coloring vector shapes. I almost never work on two drawings at a time.

LIBERTAD, 2010

Camilla, 2011

Venice Carnival, 2009

Slua Bloody Mary, 2010

GODDESS AUTUMN, 2009

Sharon Milne

"I love nothing more than getting consumed in an illustration."

RUNNING, 2012

For most of my illustrations, I start with stock images as a reference to draw basic shapes and shading, and then I build upon the foundations with detailing, highlights, deep shadow, and texturing. Sometimes I'll sketch digitally in Adobe Photoshop and then find stock images to help build a guide, or I'll use a stock image as the initial inspiration and then work from there in Illustrator. I've never hidden my use of stock images from people who follow my work and tutorials; I think it helps make my tutorials more accessible—when starting out, you don't need to know how to draw, just how to follow a photo stock image.

When working on a personal illustration, my inspiration comes from two sources: If I'm creating an animal illustration, the concept origi-nates from the behaviors of my pets. My two cats and dog are color-ful characters, and their personalities help me tell a story. My biggest influences for my portrait work are drag queens. In illustration, you tend to exaggerate emotions and appearances to ensure your story is communicated clearly to your viewer. Drag queens tend to be over the top in their appearance—big hair, bold makeup, bright colors, they all fit into place in my portrait illustrations.

I love nothing more than getting consumed in an illustration. I tend to go overboard at times and pack in as much detail as I can in my portrait work. Because I can zoom in up to 6400% with Illustrator, I find myself adding details you wouldn't necessarily see in a standard print or web graphic. These details are really for my enjoyment only; I get to see the artwork so close up and can appreciate vector as a truly infinitely scalable medium.

GREEN, 2012

PSYCHEDELIC, FUNKY, 2012

► Nom, 2010

Murder Scene, 2010

Leo the Lion, 2011

Using a Stock Base to Create a Playful Cat Illustration

My pets often inspire my animal illustrations, and this one is no exception. As do most cats, mine loves chasing flies, so why not turn my Harley into a pop culture icon while she's chasing one? In this Adobe Illustrator tutorial, I'll show you how I've created this illustration from a sketch and stock image, in my own cat's colors.

1 **Sketching the Concept**

Using the Blob Brush Tool (Shift+B), I sketch the concept I have in mind. The idea is to have the cat coming out of darkness, so I only want to illustrate the key features of her face, her paw holding the chopsticks, and the fly. I then use the Line Segment Tool (\) to draw the chopsticks with Round Caps and the Width Tool (Shift+W) to increase the Stroke Weight toward the top of the chopsticks.

2 **Placing the Stock Image**

Next, I purchase a stock image of a cat with the pose I want to use. I choose File > Place to place that image onto the Artboard, where I also place an image of my cat so I can easily refer to it. I draw additional details with the Blob Brush Tool (Shift+B) for the eyes, because I wish to achieve a cartoon look in the final illustration.

❸ Using Gradients as a Fur Base

I add a square with an off black/brown fill with the Rectangle Tool (M). I begin to build up the areas of color on Harley's face and paw using transparent radial gradients. I use the Eyedropper Tool (I) to sample colors from her reference image. I then set these gradients to Blending Mode Screen with an Opacity of 5% to 15% (depending on how bold I want to have the colors). I draw these shapes using the Pencil Tool (N).

❹ Creating an Art Brush

In this step, I draw a black fill flat circle with the Ellipse Tool (L) and use the Convert Anchor Point Tool (Shift+C) to pinch the sides of the shape. Then in the Brush panel I choose Add Brush > New Art Brush. For the Colorization Method, I select Tints.

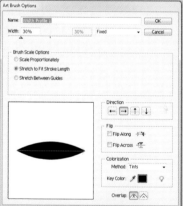

❺ Starting the Fur

I then use the Paintbrush Tool (B) with my new Art Brush to draw short strands of fur, working with the colors used within the transparent radial gradients. I set these strokes to Blending Mode Normal and Opacity 30%–50%, again depending on the placements and how bold I want to have the colors. I've also paid attention to my Harley reference image to make sure the fur is going in the correct direction.

6 Adding Definition

I add strokes around the lighter areas and set the strokes to Blending Mode Screen and Color Dodge to add further highlights and contrast. I add darker strokes with a gray/brown stroke color. These strokes are set to Blending Mode Multiply with an Opacity of 50%–80%. These help shape the fur patches. I've also added strokes to define the paw that will hold the chopsticks.

7 Adding Facial Feature Bases

Using the Pen Tool (P), I draw base shapes for the eyes and nose. The eyes consist of two shapes each, one off-black/brown for the inner eye and one for the eyeball. Based on the contrast they've produced, I decide to add more transparent radial gradients to help soften the strokes. I also add some more contrast against the off-black background.

8 Using Gradients on the Features

In the Appearance panel for the shapes for the eyes and nose, I add New Fills and use gradients to add variety in color and shape to the features. Using the Gradient Tool (G), I reposition the gradient source. I use the Ellipse Tool (L) to add pupils to the eyes and then a pale, inverted transparent radial gradient to add a shine to the eyes. I then use the Pencil Tool (N) to add further shapes to the fur and around the eyes to add more depth with brown transparent radial gradients.

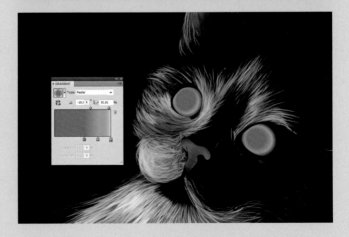

I use the same chopsticks used in the sketch, but this time I reposition them. I use Pathfinder > Minus Front to create the shape I need (minus the paw). I then use a duplicate of the chopsticks in a Compound Path (Ctrl+8) and then a Clipping Mask (Ctrl+7) to add gradients for shadows cast by the paws. Because Harley is a different breed from the cat in the stock image, I use the Lasso Tool (Q) to select sections of the face and then the Free Transform Tool (E) to resize and reposition the snout and side of her face.

⑩ **Finishing the Chopsticks**

More gradients are used within the chopstick Clipping Mask as well as detailing for the ends of the sticks. I draw a rough sketch of a fly in the direction of Harley's eyes so I know where to draw next.

⑪ **Drawing a Quick Fly**

I create the fly with two Ellipses (L) and use rough scribbles for the wings. I then use the Pen Tool (P) to draw a random curved line for the path the fly has flown. This approach adds to the cartoon look of the illustration but also helps show that the fly is moving.

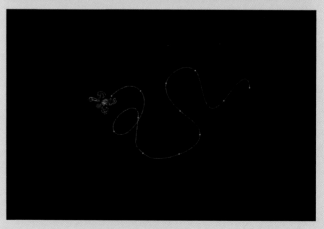

12 Modifying the Face Contouring

I add further strokes around the face set to Blending Mode Screen. My goal is to emphasize the slim face Harley has, with her more pronounced cheekbones. I add highlights around the eyes and also around the lower lip (so it's not lost in the illustration). And adding fine whiskers is essential if you're drawing a cat!

13 Finishing Touches

Finally, I add two Ellipses (L) per eye for a reflection of light and then fine lines around the waterline and corner of the eye. This helps give the eyes "life" and character. I finish off the illustration by using the Artboard Tool (Shift+O) to reposition the Artboard crop so I have the right composition.

Conclusion

I hope you've enjoyed this cat illustration tutorial and can see how using a mixture of transparent gradients with the Pencil Tool (N) and a custom Art Brush with the Paintbrush Tool (B) can lend a soft edge to an otherwise hard-edged vector composition.

Junichi Tsuneoka

"I established a style...California Roll Stylie...a visual and conceptual fusion of Japanese pop culture and American urban culture."

DREAMCATCHER, 2011

I was born in Japan and spent most of my time there until I came to the U.S. to be a designer. Based on my background and my experiences, I established a style often recognized as *California Roll Stylie*, the result of both a visual and conceptual fusion of Japanese pop culture and American urban culture. I founded Studio Stubborn Sideburn to broaden my visual communication and employ my visual language in art, illustration, and design. My pieces possess highly communicative, assertive graphics, and contain clear signs pointing back to my background.

I often think of my creative process as two parts. It starts as spontaneous drawings. I draw whatever I have in my mind first, based on the concept of the project. This is more like doodling. After doing so for a while, I start looking at the drawing as a design. That means that I digest the drawing, simplify it, exaggerate, add things, and so on. This second part of the process is carefully calculated and time-consuming, compared to the spontaneous first part. At the same time, these two processes are important to each other. If one is incomplete, then I will not be satisfied with the result of the design at the end. Everything I design goes through these phases, and I do enjoy both parts of the process in different ways.

▶ BASSNECTAR, 2012

KID CUDI, 2011

REPTAR, 2012

MOS DEF, 2010

SPARKLY, 2011

Rubens Cantuni

"I always try to push the curiosity in the viewers, making them ask themselves questions about what they're seeing."

REALMAC LOGO REMIX, 2011

Having tons of interests, from Asian cultures to street and pop art, tattoos, movies, videogames, and comics, I've found a way to push all these into a multiflavored art style. Probably one of the main characteristics of my work can be summed up in the word *contrast*. Childish yet disturbing, funny and sexy, sharp but curvy, and ironic. I always try to push the curiosity in the viewers, making them ask themselves questions about what they're seeing. Maybe they won't find the answers, but they'll be amused. At least that's what I hope.

My personal advice to new artists is that making your own stuff is always worth the hard work. It's never a waste of time.

SWEET NIGHTMARE, 2010

4 OF CLUBS, 2012

5 OF SPADES, 2012

NIKE OCTOPUS, 2011

COSMIC WHEELIE, 2012

Jared Nickerson

"I always try to interject small bits of humor into my work."

I work primarily in Adobe Illustrator CS5, as my main medium is 2D vector. This format translates easily onto everything from textile, video, and animation, and miscellaneous print projects. My main focus is character, logo, video game, editorial, and textile design. I also do art direction, branding and consulting. I specialize in characters that aren't direct references to pop culture but are often inspired by various pop-culture entities from the last 60 years, including Disney and Hanna-Barbera. I've also become known for an "editorial style" portrait, which I first developed while working with Suicide Girls.

I don't have a specific message I want people to walk away with after viewing my artwork. Most of my artwork is purely for "visual" sake. However, I always try to interject small bits of humor into my work. My motto is create art for yourself and in time everyone else will follow.

GEOMAGNETIC XRAY
SPECS, 2010

WHEN ENTROPY FALLS, 2010

GO TO SLEEP CITIZEN, 2010

THE LAST VAMPIRE ASTRONAUT, 2011

Using a Limited Palette and Bold Line Art to Create a Character with Attitude

In this tutorial I'll show you how to use Adobe Illustrator to create a character that oozes attitude, using a limited palette and bold line art. You'll start with basic shapes and then add minor details to give your drawing a professional finish.

1 Starting with Four Ellipses

Draw the beginning of your character using four ellipses created with the Ellipse Tool (L): one for the head, one for the body, and two for the wings on either side. Try to keep them as symmetrical as possible by using options in the Align panel.

2 Building on Your Base Shapes

Apply a thick outline to the ellipses and use the Add Anchor Point Tool (+) and Direct Selection Tool (A) to modify the wings' shape. Create an eye and duplicate it; then use Transform > Reflect to mirror-copy the eye. Create a beak shape with the Pen Tool (P).

3 Giving Him Character

Add features such as hands, feet, head detailing, and shape. Here I've used tapered lines for the hand detailing and darkened the gray fill in the head so it stands out more from the body.

4 Adding Texture with Lines

This step involved adding more detail, such as creases in feather and fur, detailing in the hair and feathers, and general eye enhancement. Use tapered lines again to create a feather/fur texture and to also lend detailing to the beak. Add light reflections to the eyes to give them more life.

⑤ Adding Accessories

Add other primary elements such as a toothpick, a chain, and a baseball bat to help mold the character's personality and setting. Although the bird alone projects attitude, the accessories help give him character.

⑥ Creating More Attitude

Adjust the eyes and facial features to reflect the message you want your character to convey. Add eyebrows and external eye detailing. I used the Pen Tool (P) and chose Pathfinder > Unite to combine the shapes.

⑦ Texture and Shading

Return to the core shapes and elements, and start adding detailing through color. For the bird, you accomplish this mainly in the plumage and the accessory (the baseball bat). I've used varied Stroke Weights for the wood texture to give it a more organic feel.

⑧ Working on the Background Elements

Don't neglect the world around your character, where he lives, who his friends are (if any), what he interacts with regularly. Trees seemed the obvious choice in this scenario. I fleshed them out just like the core character, using tapered lines and a limited palette.

⑨ Building a Composition

In this step, you place the supporting background objects until you've decided it's enough—in this case, supporting typography, clouds, moon, additional trees, and a nail in the bat. I don't use black on the lines in the background, because it would distract from the character. The purpose of the background is to support the character and not to take away the attention of the viewer.

⑩ Minor Details and Highlights

In the final step you apply shading, highlights, and any final detailing and touchups such as a rough patch on the head, a white outline around the core character, and so forth. Things like these help the character stand out further.

Conclusion

With the effective use of bold line art and minor details, you can help your character stand out. This illustration would be great as a mascot or even as a t-shirt design. The benefits of a limited color palette are that it's easier for you to alter colors and discover which would be best for your project.

Nabhan Abdullatif

I'm a graphic artist and illustrator from the Sultanate of Oman in the Middle East. I started drawing at the age of eight and pursued it as a career choice when I decided to study graphic design in college.

My love affair with Adobe Illustrator started in 2005 when I switched to digital media, and I have been using it ever since to create all my art pieces and conceptual designs. It provided me with the exact tools I was looking for in order to convey my concepts and ideas into a visual format. My favorite and most used Illustrator tools include the Pen, Pencil, Warp, and Brush tools.

I draw inspiration for my pieces from life surroundings and personal experiences. I look out for the symbolism in any object I see and try to create scenarios that people can relate to. The extremely positive reaction to my pieces in online communities such as DeviantArt and Facebook were definitely my motivation to keep on experimenting and to keep on creating pieces that either put a smile on people's faces or make them reflect on life and see things with a different and fresh perspective.

LISTEN, 2011

▶ MOBILE WORLD, 2010

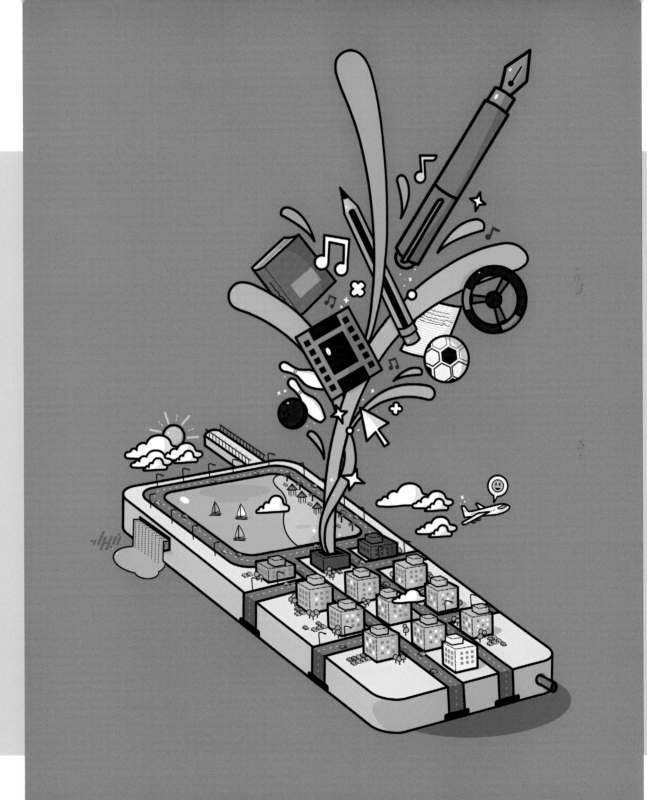

HOMELESS, 2012

NEUTRAL, 2012

COFFEE-HOLIC, 2012

HOT CHOCOLATE,
2009

Scott Bartlett

"The Pen Tool was some black voodoo magic that I just couldn't grasp."

SKATEBOARDS, 2012

When I first began learning how to work with vectors in Illustrator, I detested them. Just the thought of going to class to learn how to use Illustrator put me in a bad mood. The Pen Tool was some black voodoo magic that I just couldn't grasp. I kept asking classmates for help again and again, but it just wasn't sinking in. I felt like a failed designer. It wasn't until about two months in that something finally clicked and it all made sense. That was an amazing experience. I started churning out vectors left and right. My friends who had been teaching me were now asking me for help. I haven't gone more than a week of my life since without booting up Illustrator.

I entered a 7-Eleven design competition a few years back; the winning design would be printed on t-shirts and handed out all over Australia. My vector piece took the top prize, and now, more than three years later, I still see people around town wearing my design. It makes me smile.

OctoArts, 2012

Vector Stickers, 2010-2012

SKULL EMBLEM, 2011

VECTOR TATTOOS, 2012

YETI GAMER, 2012

Mary Winkler

"My work is...often childlike in theme, depicting sweets, fanciful creatures, and rainbows."

CAKES 'N' CREAM, 2008

My work is vivid and whimsical. It's often childlike in theme, depicting sweets, fanciful creatures, and rainbows, as well as exploring the world of fashion and garment in illustrated form. Done in a variety of media, including digital, acrylic, watercolor, and ink, it's pop art, graphic, and—for lack of a better word—sparkly.

My work is painted on canvas, a variety of papers, or printed by way of giclée inkjet or silkscreen, usually onto fabric for pouches/bags. I studied illustration at College for Creative Studies in Detroit, Michigan.

Orange Watermelon Raspberry, 2011

PLASTIC DJ, 2012

SUNDAE DARLING, 2007

GHOSTS OF ME, GHOSTS OF YOU, 2012

Creating a Cheerfully Colorful Fish Illustration from a Sketch

Greetings, color kids. Acrylicana here to give a peek behind the curtain in creating some bright, bold, and poster-style illustrations. Primarily, I use the Pen Tool (N), Pencil Tool (M), and Gradient Tools (G). Throw a few more into the mix, and we've got a finished piece. Let's do this!

1 **Using Basic Shapes to Trace the Sketch**

After doodling a sketch in Adobe Photoshop, I pop it into Illustrator (File > Place) in a new document that's print-ready at 300dpi and CMYK. Then I start out with basic shapes and the Pen Tool (P). This lets me play with my color palette and map out the composition, in case my sketch isn't working for the final image.

2 **Creating a Candy Swirl**

Some details, like the candy swirl, are easiest to do with the Pencil Tool (N). Just create the shape you think works best, keeping the forced perspective of the candy in mind while doing so.

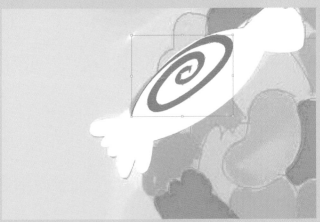

140

❸ Balancing Your Composition with Base Shapes

All shapes are now created. I'm not sure if this fish and candy is underwater or in space. I don't think it really matters as long as the design fits the right aesthetic.

❹ Adding Small Details with the Pen Tool

This step involves adding little details on the fish with the Pen Tool (P). I'm sticking with solid colors in this piece (for the most part). Create some depth with a dark orange on the fin and let the top part of the eye *pop* with a yellow-orange as you see fit.

❺ Adding Shapes and Modifying the Opacity

I add the same color to the fins. They seem a bit too bright for me, though, so I open the Transparency panel and reduce the Opacity setting on both shapes.

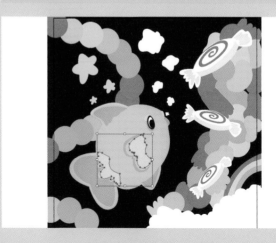

6 **Adding Varied Outlines**

Time to add some outlines to the shapes. Instead of applying a Stroke, I like to Copy and Paste the main shape behind itself (use Pathfinder to Unite this "shadow"). The dark shape has a Stroke Weight of 2pt and the white one has a Stroke Weight of 6pt. Repeat with the candies. In this case I want to keep more focus on the fish and other things in the piece, so the candies will receive only a thin dark outline.

7 **Using Gradients for Rays in the Background**

In this step I add some sunray-like shapes to the background of the piece. The Gradient is the same as the background itself, but reversed (one is at 90 degrees, the other −90). If you find this too harsh, reduce the Opacity of the shape outline.

8 **Creating a Simple Shadow Effect**

Add a Gradient fill shape to make the fish shiny. Add as well some simple Drop Shadow shapes behind the fish and candies.

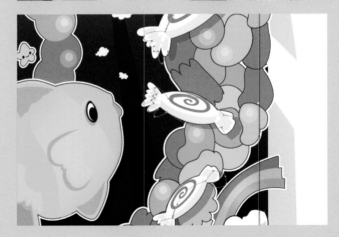

⑨ Start Creating a Rainbow

I like my rainbows to pop. I start with a simple outlined color. In this case, it's the same as the fish outline: dark to light.

⑩ Finishing the Rainbow

The rainbow (or any shape, really) is aligned on top. This is a group of three shapes. I make a big to-do of this step simply to show that grouping shapes makes everything so much easier and organized.

⑪ Adding a Shine to the Rainbow

To make the rainbows shiny, I Copy the shapes, use Pathfinder to Unite, and apply a radial gradient including white, pink, and purple. The exact shades vary, but it's my go-to technique for making elements smooth and slightly rendered. Reduce the Opacity as you see fit so the rainbow colors pop through.

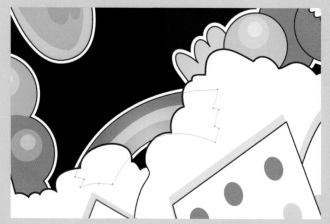

⑫ Refining the Details
Dissatisfied with the blobby cloud shapes the fish was making, I delete part of them and redraw some other blobs with the Pencil Tool (N). Make as many changes from the original sketch as you see fit.

⑬ Modifying the Background
The sunrays in the background still seem harsh as a gradient, so I change them to a light blue (with Opacity reduced to 30%). I want the background to have some interest, but not to overwhelm the rest of the piece, as it's all very bold and coloring book–like.

Conclusion

This piece is fun, bright, and bold. I like to pop out poster designs that are reminiscent of my childhood without rendering each element too much (although once you start playing with gradients, it's hard to stop—they're awfully pretty).

McKelly

"We were drawn to each other via our shared love of comics, animation, illustration, and, of course, vector."

Discovering Melbourne, 2008

We are Kate McInnes and Sean Kelly, a collaborative creative duo known as McKelly. With a penchant for the provocative, our style could be described as "Miss Universe meets the Apocalypse."

We were drawn to each other via our shared love of comics, animation, illustration, and, of course, vector. Drawing inspiration from pop culture, politics, and current events, our artwork is born from a constant creative tête-à-tête. We have a truly collaborative process. First comes the concept and then the sketch stage. This generally begins on paper but quickly moves to digital as we draw over each other's work and share working documents between computers. This working tennis game progresses to the finished art stage: generally Kate takes control of direction and color, and Sean does the digital inking.

McKelly formed naturally as a result of our working side by side in many Australian exhibitions. This culminated in the Suit Up project, which produced a limited-edition, all-Australian-artist deck of playing cards. Since then we have continued to explore vector illustration and screen printing techniques, as well as branching into animation and video installation work. Our work is seen on skate decks, snowboards, sticker collections, t-shirts, toys, tattoos, and limited-edition prints.

▶ Fight Like Rabbits, 2009

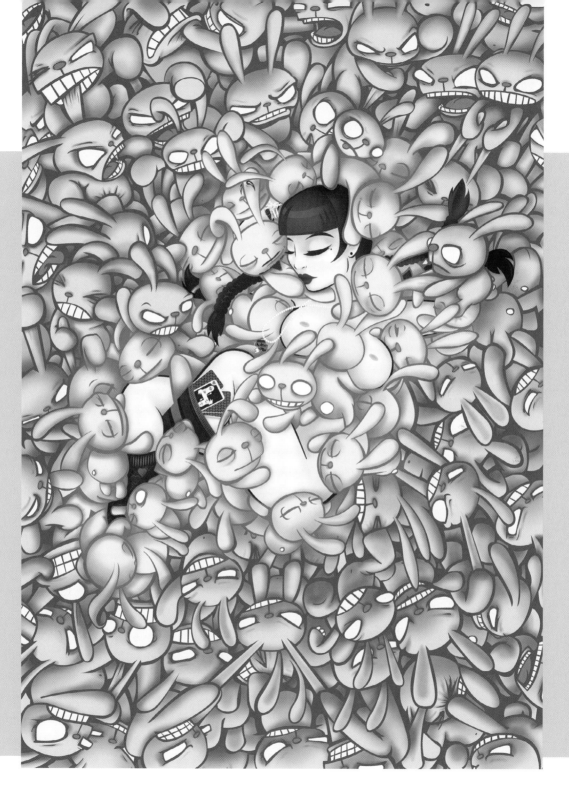

SATYR OF CORRUPTION, 2009

SIREN OF POWER, 2009

OBSOLESCENCE, 2011

A Very Bogan
Christmas, 2009

Roberlan Borges

"When something makes me stop and think, I try to bring to paper every detail that I remember."

SYMMETRY – SELF PORTRAIT, 2012

Since I started drawing, I've observed a lot of aspects that I believe are a good mix of inspirations and influences: vintage style, pop culture, music, cinema, games, and politics, for example. Of course, there are also other artists who push me to try, like Simon Bisley, Brian Brasher, Arthur Saron Sarnoff, Gil Elvgren, Moebius, Keith Haring, Roy Lichenstein, Jim Flora, and Alphonse Mucha.

I choose some moments and movements of world history to expose particular characteristics that I think are interesting points of view, like smiles, haircuts, body position, eyes, and female muses.

My vector artwork also has some influences of Art Nouveau, cyberculture/cyberpunk, humor, and satire. Nowadays, as a creative professional working as an art director and illustrator, when something makes me stop and think, I try to bring to paper every detail that I remember, like colors, light, curves, lettering, and font styles. After that, it is time to start the creative journey full of changes, some mistakes, and, with a little bit of luck and hard work, success.

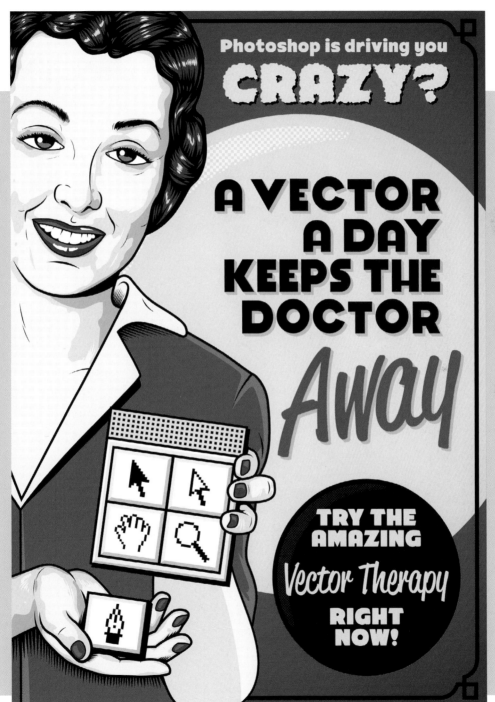

SQUARETOWN, 2011

IMPOSSIBLE LOVE, 2012

LOLLIPOP, 2012

A KIWI A DAY, 2012

Cristiano Siqueira

"I like to work in the details and the precision of the lines."

I'm an illustrator from São Paulo, Brazil, and I'm also known by the artistic identity CrisVector. I have developed an illustration technique using vectors—always in Adobe Illustrator—and I like to work in the details and the precision of the lines.

My main source of inspiration contributing to my illustration style is comics, especially classic illustrations using black ink and flat colors. Having studied fine art, I also drew inspiration from classical art movements such Pop Art, Surrealism, and Expressionism.

On the professional side, I started my career working first as graphic designer for books, CD covers, magazines, and posters. Later on I worked as an art director in packaging design for toys and food products.

▸ EDGAR ALLAN POE, 2011

LIONEL MESSI, 2010

Le Chapeau Noir, 2008

Communion, 2007

MATADORA, 2009

KRYSTAL, 2007

From Photo to Finish, Creating a Stylish Self-Portrait

In this tutorial, I show you my process of creating an illustration based on a photo. Adobe Photoshop is used to prepare the source image and the illustration is created using Adobe Illustrator. I use a graphic tablet with the Paintbrush Tool (B), taking advantage of the default Calligraphic Brushes with a touch of personal customization. In this way I can simulate the inking you see done in comics. Let's begin!

1 Preparing the Document

Open the source image in Adobe Illustrator. Make sure the file is in CMYK mode (to check it, choose Menu > File > Document Color Mode > CMYK). Since I always work with solid colors, I like to work from scratch in CMYK. Choose File > Place to put the image on your Artboard. Set the Opacity of the image to 30% and lock the layer.

2 Preparing to Create Line Art

Create a new layer and name it "Linework." I start off with the Pen Tool (P), using a rich black. (My "black" has percentages of other colors in it. Mine are C 40, M 30, Y 30, B 100.) I make my illustrations in two basic stages: head and body. Start with the head/face since it's the main focus of the illustration and thus demands great attention to detail.

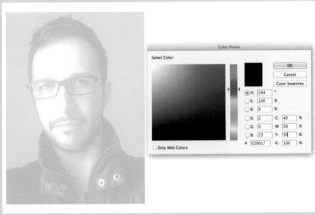

❸ Starting with Facial Features

In this step, you use the Pen Tool (P) to detail the eyes, mouth, nose, and the glasses. You can then move on to make the full linework using the Paintbrush Tool (B) and the Pen Tool (P). To enjoy the maximum precision the Pen Tool (P) has to offer, draw the shapes using the fewest anchor points possible, using the curves more than the points. The pupil and iris of the eye can be done with the Ellipse Tool (L).

❹ Using the Pencil Tool

To draw the hair, use the Pencil Tool (N). Double-click the tool to define the setup; I set mine to Fidelity: 2.5px and Smoothness: 0%.

❺ Drawing the Hair

For the hair, start off by shaping out the darker areas with the Pencil Tool (N). Then select the Paintbrush Tool (B) to finish it off.

6 Modifying a Default Brush

A large part of this illustration will be done with brushes, so it's important to customize some Calligraphic Brushes offered in Illustrator. I have a set with some brushes that I use to do almost everything. My setup for a basic brush is Angle: −41° Fixed (no variation), Roundness: 35% with variation of Pressure (to use the pressure variation of the tablet), variation of 20%, and Diameter: 3pt, pressure variation of 3pt.

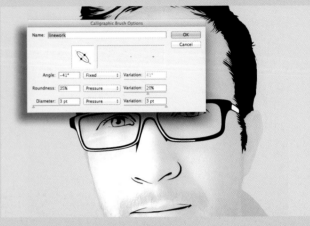

7 Adding Line Detailing for Contouring and Fine Hair

Using your customized brushes, begin drawing the lines of the face, starting with the main face features and moving to the details and midtones. This time the process is more organic; it's more drawing technique than software technique. You can change the Opacity of the base image to 60% so you can see more details.

8 Finishing the Line Art

Now you have the linework of the face completed. Repeat some of the previous steps to draw the jacket; first the black areas, then the lines and details for a finish. Next you can begin coloring.

⑨ Adding Base Colors

Create a new layer, name it "Colors," and place it under the Linework layer. Set the Linework layer to Blending Mode Multiply, lock it, and then click on the Colors layer. Use the Pen Tool (P) to add in a gray shape for a base (different shades of gray are used on the eyes).

⑩ Comparing the Illustration to the Photo

With the Pen Tool (P) and/or Pencil Tool (N), draw the first shades of the skin, using the original photograph as a guide. I tend to make the shade about 5% darker than the original photograph. Use a copy of the first shape to cut and fit the shading levels. Copy and paste it onto the same spot (Ctrl+C and Ctrl+F); after selecting both, use the Intersect option in the Pathfinder panel.

⑪ Adding Depth

Add three more shades of gray to add to the shadow work (each 5% darker than the last).

12 **Adding Highlights and a Backlight Effect**

To finish, you add the highlights. You started with a very light gray, so the highlights can be about 3% lighter than the base color. Add shapes of highlights in special and unusual places to achieve an interesting effect. The final touch can be some white shapes on the border of the face; this lends a "backlight" effect to the illustration. The same procedure you used for the skin can be used for the jacket. Here I used only one layer of shading and several for highlights.

13 **Finishing the Composition**

For the final step, add a subtle background tone to help the illustration stand out.

Conclusion

My aim is not to be hyper-realistic, but I want the final work to be related to the source image and, at the same time, I'm looking for a comic-style illustration. By experimenting on your own photographs, you can allow yourself to make mistakes and take your time to learn new skills and styles. If in the end you have a creative self-portrait, then that's a bonus!

Beto Garza

"My inspiration has and will always be cartoons, comic books, and videogames."

I've always loved drawing. As a kid I was always doodling with crayons all over my house walls, and now it is my line of work professionally. But for me drawing is more than just a profession because it lets me express myself about anything I want to and to be fully satisfied. My inspiration has and will always be cartoons, comic books, and videogames.

I like to use geometrical and mechanical shapes in my vector art, and I also like plain rough colors. Back in college I realized that I could do a whole illustration composed of only geometrical figures—something that would be harder to achieve by sketching by hand using pencil and paper. It is very important to constantly keep experimenting with new techniques. I prefer to maintain a separation between my vector art and the other media that I use, such as ink, watercolor, or acrylic; they are whole different universes from each other.

Ma Ma Ma, 2009

▶ Donevecha, 2012

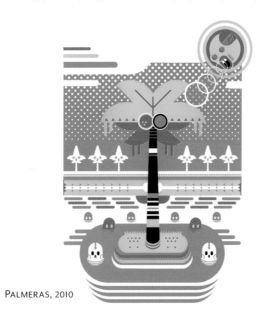

PALMERAS, 2010

CACAHUATE Y BOSES, 2012

▶ HASTA MORIR, 2012

CALAVERAS Y DIABLITOS, 2010

Ivan Petrushevski

"Illustration is a field of endless possibilities once you get rid of the classical rules and aesthetics of traditional art."

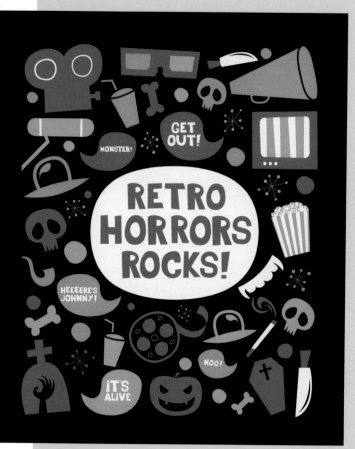

RETRO HORRORS ROCK, 2008

My works are mainly influenced by J-Pop (a Japanese pop music genre), vintage illustration, and street art. I don't over-think the outcome of my illustrations; I merely start with something and wait to see what will happen at the end of the process. Illustration is a field of endless possibilities once you get rid of the classical rules and aesthetics of traditional art.

My palette often contains warm, vibrant colors and is limited to few of them. Using few colors and lots of details can make the work seem complex yet simple at the same time. Creating images that come only from a pure creative impulse and without any general meaning or ideology behind them is a typical childish behavior. That's exactly what I like about my work, letting the inner kid create limitlessly whatever it wants, and I hope that this process will go on for a while.

▶ OLD OLD SCHOOL, 2011

WINTER, 2011

THE LONELY GIANT, 2008

MONSTER - CONFUSED, 2011

MR. NOVEMBER, 2011

Michelle Romo

"I want to make you something that is going to be your favorite thing!"

PANDAROO, 2012

I am a self-taught illustrator and designer who is fueled by cookies and naps. Influences for my work include Japanese and Scandinavian design and pretty much anything cute. The main message behind my work is sweetness and love. I want to make you something that is going to be your favorite thing!

In 2004, I started designing under the name Crowded Teeth. Crowded Teeth is a whimsical, sweet line of characters with a bold, fresh graphic influence. Created with an eye-pleasing color palette and a fun sense of humor, the designs appeal to all ages.

When I'm not working, I spend my time eating good food, hugging my friends, playing video games, and crafting. Currently I reside in Los Angeles with my super awesome husband Jason and our two cats, Hurts and Morgan.

▶ SUPER AWESOME SWEET RAD TIMES AT FUZZY MOUNTAIN: HECK YEAH, 2010

It Flamin-goes, 2012

Giraffe Love, 2010

Magical Elephant, 2012

I Love You ... Me Too, 2012

Recycling Simple Shapes to Create a Fun Camera Illustration

In this tutorial, I'll explain how to draw a camera with cute little blob guys. The purpose is to show that you can create great graphics using even the most basic tools. I like to repeat shapes within my artwork, so I'll also demonstrates how to use the same shapes to create different elements of a drawing. For example, the blob guys' bodies are the same shape used in the brush around the lens. Repeating elements visually tie the graphic together.

① Starting with a Simple Shape

Start by using the Ellipse Tool (L). Set the measurements to 1.5 in x 1.5 in.

Use the Direct Selection Tool (A) to pull the top point upward, and pull the handles to the left and right of the top point to create your blob friend. I like mine to look a little uneven so it has a more handmade feel.

② Splitting the Shape

Use the Line Segment Tool (/) to create a 2 in horizontal line with no fill and no stroke across the middle of your blob friend. Using the Selection Tool (V), select the line and blob shape; then in the Pathfinder panel, use Divide to break apart the pieces.

3. Deleting and Making Minor Adjustments

Ungroup (Shift+Command+G) the pieces and delete the bottom section. Using the Direct Selection Tool (A), pull the bottom line of the blob to create your desired shape.

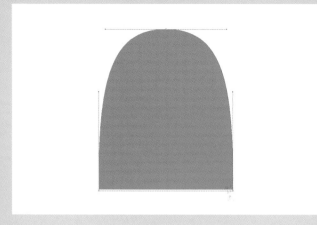

4. Adding Features

Use the Ellipse Tool (L) to create circles for the eyes (0.06 in) and cheeks (0.125 in). Create an oval for the mouth (0.3 in x 0.05 in), and from the Effect drop-down menu, choose Warp > Arc. Set the bend to –25% to create a little smile.

5. Duplicate and Recolor

Group (Command+G) all pieces of the blob. Copy (Command+C) and paste (Command+V) two instances of the blob. Recolor so that your blob guy has a variety of friends.

6 **Creating the Camera Base**

Use the Rectangle Tool (M) to create the body of the camera. Set the measurements to 5.25 in x 3.6 in.

7 **Creating a Pattern Brush**

Now you are going to start on the lens of the camera. Copy (Command+C) and paste (Command+V) the red blob friend, and ungroup (Shift+Command+G) the pieces. Drag the main body piece into the Brush panel and create a New Pattern Brush. Set Scale to 50% and Spacing to 100%.

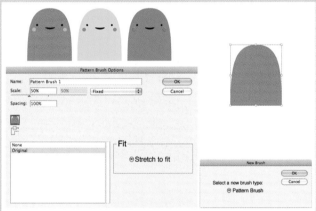

8 **Applying a Brush to the Lens**

Using the Ellipse Tool (L), create a circle that is 1.75 in x 1.75 in, add the Pattern Brush you just created to the ellipse, and set the Stroke Weight to 0.15 pts.

⑨ Adding Lens Detail

Using the Ellipse Tool (L), create a 1.35 in x 1.35 in circle. Add a blue fill and a 3pt white stroke. Create a 2.3 in x 2.3 in circle. Add a black fill and a 3pt basic white stroke. Then send this backward so that it is behind the previously made red and blue pieces.

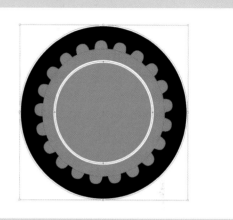

⑩ Adding Facial Features

Using the Selection Tool (V), select all of these pieces. Open the Align panel and click the Horizontal Align Center and Vertical Align Center buttons. Copy (Command+C) and paste (Command+V) the face you created for the blob and place it on the lens. Using the Ellipse Tool (L), create 0.4 in x 0.4 in circle to use as a highlight on the lens.

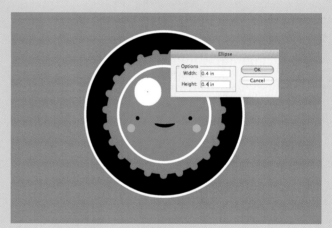

⑪ Modifying a Rectangle to Form a Pattern

Using the Rectangle Tool (M), create a 0.5 in x 1 in rectangle with a dark red fill. Create two more rectangular pieces that are 0.1 in x 1 in. Use the Direct Selection Tool (A) to pull on the top and bottom points horizontally to create imperfect rectangles. Make sure you just move the points left and right, not up or down.

12 **Creating a Pattern Brush and Applying**

Group (Command+G) these three pieces and drag them into the Brush panel. Set the scale to 100% and the spacing to 0%. Create a 2 in x 2 in circle using the Ellipse Tool (L), and apply the brush you just made to it with a 0.5 in Stroke Weigh t. Send this backward (Command+[) until it's behind the other pieces of the lens that you previously made.

13 **Creating the Viewfinder**

Now you're going to make the viewfinder on the camera. Using the Ellipse Tool (L), create a 0.5 in x 0.5 in black circle with a 1.5 pt Stroke Weight. Then create a 0.3 in x 0.1 in oval. Using the Direct Selection Tool (A), move the points so it is slightly uneven. It should look like a rounded highlight. Select both pieces using the Selection Tool (V) and Group (Command+G) them. Place this above the lens.

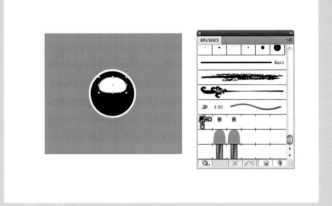

14 **Splitting a Square**

Using the Rectangle Tool (M), create a 1 in x 1 in square. Using the Line Segment Tool (\), create a line whose length is 1.25 in and at a 45 degree angle. Create a second line whose length is 1.25 in and at a 225 degree angle. Select all the pieces using the Selection Tool (V), and using the Align panel, click the Horizontal Align Center and Vertical Align Center buttons. With all pieces selected, click the Divide button in the Pathfinder panel. This will create four separate shapes from the original square. Recolor each piece a different shade of gray.

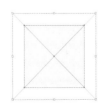

⑮ Creating a Simple Camera Button

Using the Rectangle Tool (M), create a 0.8 in x 0.2 in rectangle for the bottom section of the camera button. Then create a 0.65 in x 0.25 in rectangle for the top part. Fill both with black. Select all the pieces using the Selection Tool (V), and using the Align panel, click the Horizontal Align Center button. Send these pieces behind the main body of the camera (Command+[).

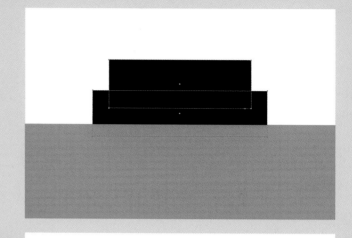

⑯ Recycling a Pattern Brush

Drag the brush you previously made out of the Brush panel and onto the workspace. Rotate this artwork 90 degrees using the Rotate Tool (R). Double-click on the Selection Tool (V) to bring up the Move menu. Set Horizontal Position to 0 and Vertical Position to 0.5 in, and select Copy.

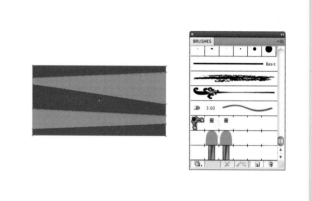

⑰ Camera Detailing

Duplicate this process five times (Command+D). Using the Selection Tool (V), select all of these pieces and set the size in the Transform panel to 1.25 in x 3.5 in (be sure that the size linking is not selected). Group these together (Command+G). Using the Selection Tool (V), select this group and the main body of the camera; then, using the Align panel, click the Horizontal Align Left and Vertical Align Top buttons.

18 Organizing Your Composition

Place your blob friends around the camera, and hide some behind the camera by sending them backward (Command+[).

19 Using Rectangles to Make a Pattern

Using the Rectangle Tool (M), create a 2 in x 0.5 in light green rectangle. Double-click on the Selection Tool (V) to bring up the Move menu. Set the horizontal position to 0 and the vertical position to 0.5 in, and select Copy. Make the copied rectangle a darker shade of green. Using the Selection Tool (V), select both pieces and group them (Command+G). Then drag them into the Swatch panel.

20 Adding the Finishing Touches

Create an 8 in x 8 in square using the Rectangle Tool (M) and send it to back (Shift+Command+[). Select all the pieces except the new background piece using the Selection Tool (V) and Group them (Command+G). Select the group and the background piece using the Selection Tool (V), and using the Align panel, click the Horizontal Align Center and Vertical Align Center buttons.

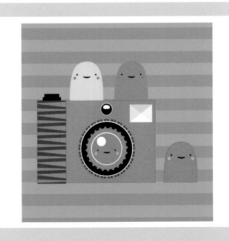

Conclusion

This graphic would be good as a t-shirt graphic, or any kind of product that can feature a printed or embroidered floating graphic. Also, since it is simple with big shapes and bold colors, it could be used for an icon or other small web graphic.

Sometimes I can get carried away trying to be extra fancy in my designs, but it's good to remember that the simplest tools and most basic shapes make for excellent designs!

Petros Afshar

"I've always been fond of the idea of shapes, lines, small elements that combine and develop into something bigger."

My design approach has always been disciplinary and focused on experimentation. I've always been fond of the idea of shapes, lines, and small elements that combine and develop into something bigger. It's always been an imprint of how my medulla oblongata functions. When it comes to design, I like the elaborate little delicacies of how it was shaped and formed, rather than viewing it as an overall piece.

RSA STAMPS, 2010

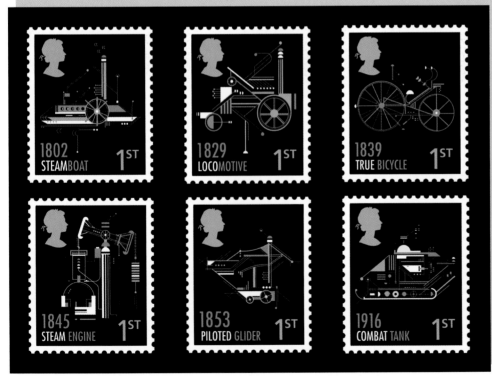

▶ CITY LIFE, 2012

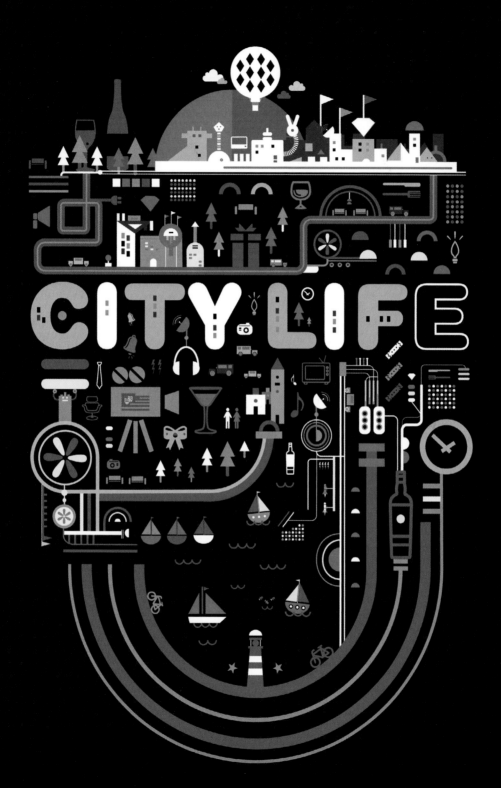

Zetter Townhouse Hotel

Spitalfield Market

Brick Lane

Victoria Park

Olympic Stadium

Tate Modern

Borough Market

N

LONDON OLYMPICS, 2012

bluejay

WEREWOLF
HOLLOW HALLOWEEN

A HERO UNSEEN   DREAMING WITHIN DREAMS

VENOM KNIGHT

· VIII . XVIII . VIIIVIII ·

INCARNATIONS OF AN
ILLUSIVE MIND

Samuel Sinaga

"I never plan my emotion. I just open Adobe Illustrator, and I'm free."

Soap, 2010

Anything and everything can be your source of inspiration—other illustration and typography, daily events, encounters with your significant others, a tragic loss, or even just one of those evenings when you stay up late to accompany your loved one and watch soap operas. Although most of the time I don't need a trigger to evoke some ideas. I like the leisure of doing art based on nothing.

I produce works that most of the time require a second look or a moment for the viewer to step back and try to understand—some time for the visual language to penetrate your mind. It's just that I never plan my emotion. I just open Adobe Illustrator, and I'm free.

Inter Action, 2010

STITZOPHRENIA, 2011

For Any Reason, 2010

Help, 2011

From Blood to the Bone, 2009

Filip Komorowski

"I was always drawing letters."

VERY HOT, 2009

I was always drawing letters. I started when I was in primary school, and that was my first encounter with graffiti. When I was in high school, my friend showed me Inkscape (an open source SVG graphics editor), and I took my first steps in vector graphics.

I'm a big fan of vintage style, and I have big collection of old postcards and newspapers. My main inspiration is classic Polish typography and design from the 60s, 70s, and 80s. There is a huge heritage for that, and it can be explored for many, many years. I like 70s and 80s music and movies—all teenage slashers and Peter Fonda movies.

Typography changed my life and I'm glad to have such a beautiful hobby.

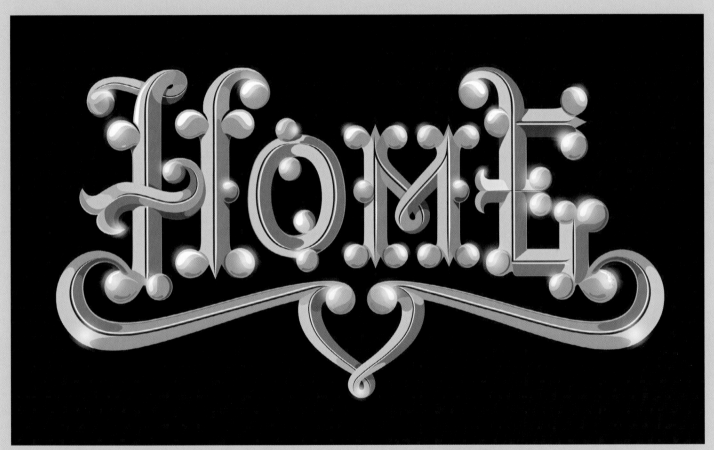

HOME, 2011

DOCTOR VECTOR, 2010

DJ SLINK, 2012

JUICY COLOR, 2012

Creating the Bulge Effect

In this tutorial I'll show you how to create the bulge effect in Adobe Illustrator and add some depth to letters in an illustration. The project used here as an example is my personal design. I did it as a tribute to 80s and 90s space arcade games and sci-fi cartoons and movies.

1 Experimenting with Styles
I always try to do many different combinations of flat, single-color letters. It's helpful to avoid problems in the steps that follow. Once I decide on the general direction of the project, I focus on one, favorite version. Here I've used the Pen Tool (P) to create the main letters.

2 Setting Widths and Direction
Verify the widths and directions of your letters, because they're the basis for any further modifications. Corrections made later in the process will cause much more additional work.

❸ Adding a 3D Style

Do some mockups. This step helps you pinpoint which option looks best. You can also quickly check whether a bold outline looks good or whether a heavy 3D effect better fits your project.

❹ Creating a 3D Effect

I use a simple technique to create this effect. Begin by duplicating the main layer, scale it, and place below your original layer. Then duplicate the main layer again and combine it with the scaled one. As a finishing touch, connect the corners using Pen Tool (P).

❺ Applying Color

Experiment with your design's colors. Working with letters can become boring; you usually work with fine details that don't change the general look of the whole project. I deal with this by mixing the colors of my project from time to time. This technique may help you discover new color schemes.

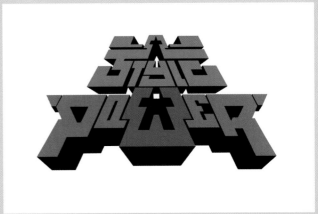

6 Adding Your First Inner Tone

Now it's time to add your first inner tone. Duplicate the main layer two times, add a stroke, turn the stroke into an object, and then, using the Pathfinder tool, cut out the stroke from the copy.

7 Adding a Second Tone

Add another tone using the same technique. Your next tone should be a bit brighter than the previous one. The only difference in this case is that this layer should fill only half of the letters.

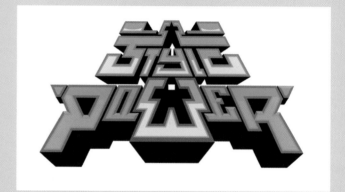

8 Using 3D Lighting to Add Depth

In this step you'll lighten the edges. Do so by using the Rectangle Tool (M). If any shapes need a specific modification, I recommend using the Pen Tool (P).

⑨ Using 3D Shadows to Add Depth

When you're done with adding light to the upper edges, it's time to add some shading to the lower ones. Do so by using the same technique described in the previous step.

⑩ Adding a Halftone Effect

This step involves adding your first halftone. You can easily create it by using the Rectangle Tool (M). Just draw a few rectangles, as shown here; combine them; and cut them out from the duplicated layer by using the Pathfinder.

⑪ Adding a Second Halftone

This step is similar to the previous one. You're just adding a halftone to the other letters. At this point you can play with various halftone widths because this effect can be used in many different ways.

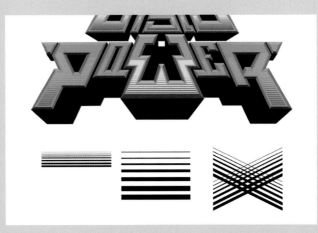

⑫ Adding Highlights

Next you can add highlights. I usually add them in the upper-right edge, but experimentation is most welcome here.

⑬ Creating an Outline

I usually add a final outline to the whole project at this point. You can do so easily by duplicating the whole project, converting it to one path, adding a stroke, and placing it below the whole project. It's a good idea to make sure all the unnecessary points were removed at this point.

⑭ Creating a Glowing Outline and Adding Flares

It's time to add the background blur in order to create a glowing outline around the whole project. The backlit project seems much heavier. Add blurred highlights in the corners. Since this is the final touch, you should decide whether the project needs any additional special effects or whether it looks better with a "pure" vector appearance.

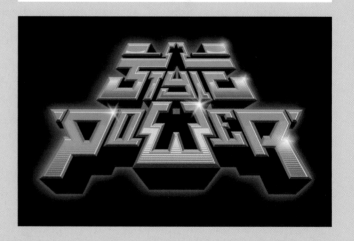

Conclusion

I like to leave my projects a couple of days and then return to them with a clear head. That way, I can spot any errors or possible modifications and enhancements. This typography style would be great to use as a poster, in a logo, or even as a standalone piece of artwork. Try it out for yourself!

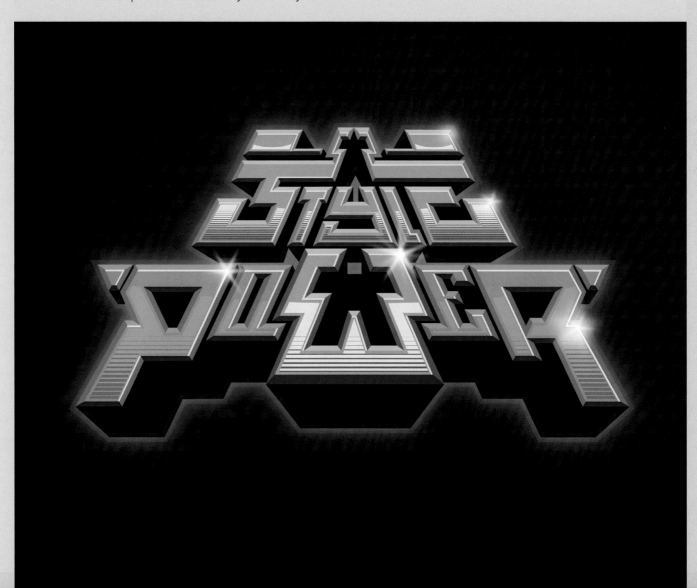

Artist Biographies

Nabhan Abdullatif

Nabhan Abdullatif is senior visualizer and illustrator for a telecom company in the Sultanate of Oman in the Middle East, where he handles advertising layout, brand structure, character design, and product packaging. See more of his artwork at: www.nabhan.devianart.com and www.nabhanabdullatif.tumblr.com.

Petros Afshar

Petros Afshar is a London-based graphic designer specializing in typography, print design, digital arts, and gardening. He owns a clothing label, and his interests span from producing music to creative writing, blogging, and organizing social events. See more of his work at: www.reanimagic.com, www.facebook.com/shoelesspeacock, and http://reanimagic.deviantart.com.

Rafael Aguilar Guzmán

Rafael Aguilar Guzmán, also known as Rafahu, is an illustrator and artist in Mexico City. After years of working for advertising agencies, he's now building his own animation and illustration studio, where he plans to make his own ideas and personal projects a reality. To see more of his work, visit: www.rafahu.com and http://rafahu.deviantart.com.

Scott Bartlett

Scott Bartlett is an illustrator and designer in Melbourne, Australia. He worked for several toy and confectionery companies before branching out to the world of freelance design. Aside from designing, Scott loves to walk around his city checking out the booming street art scene and also spends a little too much time video gaming (although he claims this is purely for inspirational purposes). See more of his work at: http://cronobreaker.deviantart.com.

Ashley S. Benson

Ashley Benson is an illustrator and vector artist residing in Phoenix, AZ. She attended Cab Calloway School of the Arts, Delaware College of Art and Design, and Pratt Institute, and she holds a Bachelor of Fine Arts with a concentration in traditional animation. Her current focus is social gaming, and she partners with Diabloskinz. See more of her work at: www.asherbee.com, http://asher-bee.daportfolio.com, and http://asher-bee.deviantart.com.

Roberlan Borges

Roberlan Borges is an art director for an advertising company in Brazil, and he works as a freelance illustrator for companies around the world. See more of his work at: www.behance.net/roberlan and http://roberlan.deviantart.com.

Rubens Cantuni

Rubens Cantuni is an illustrator and graphic designer from Genoa, Italy. He is co-founder and editor of the web magazine koikoikoi.com. See more of his work at: http://tokyocandies.com and http://tokyocandies.deviantart.com.

Charlene Chua

Charlene Chua spent her youth in Singapore, where she divided her time between drawing, reading comics, and failing her Mandarin classes. She has worked as a web designer, graphic designer, web producer, and interactive project manager. She pursued her full-time illustration career in 2006. She now lives in Canada with her husband and cat, Uno. See more of her work at: www.charlenechua.com and http://charlenechua.tumblr.com.

Justin Currie

Justin Currie is an illustrator and graphic designer from Winnipeg, Manitoba. He works for a game studio as a concept artist. See more of his work at: http://chasingartwork.deviantart.com.

Ekaterina Dedova

Ekaterina Dedova is a freelance illustrator for magazines, web, and videogames. She was born in Russia and currently lives in Italy with her family. She is now illustrating her second children's book. To see more of her work, visit: www.zzanthia.deviantart.com and http://zzzanthia.livejournal.com.

Maria Dimova

Maria Dimova is an illustrator from the Republic of Moldova. She specializes in creating vector artworks in Adobe Illustrator. She works on her own projects, takes part in contests, and spends some of her free time drawing just for fun. Maria is fond of esoteric doctrines and the art of the Ancient East and Asia. Also she likes listening to good music (mainly classic rock and jazz), reading fantasy books, going to a movie with her friends, taking part in some sports, and spending time with her family. Find her work at: http://dimary.deviantart.com and http://di-mary.livejournal.com.

Aedel Fakhrie

Aedel Fakhrie is a graphic designer and illustrator from Depok in West Java, Indonesia. He works as a digital artist for a communication firm in Singapore. See more of Aedel's work at: http://tracelandvectorie03.deviantart.com.

Beto Garza

Beto Garza, aka Helbetico, is an illustrator and graphic designer from Nuevo León, México. He has been drawing for as long as he can remember, in vector as well as inks, watercolors, and acrylics. He now writes tutorials for Vectortuts. See more of his work at: http://helbetico.deviantart.com.

Maria Goubar

Maria Goubar, aka LimKis, works as an Illustrator in the game industry and is a comic artist. She illustrates a comic project that can be seen at http://imaglif.deviantart.com. To see more of her work, visit: http://limkis-art.com and http://limkis.deviantart.com.

Helen Huang

Helen Huang is a Los Angeles–based illustrator. Aside from her full-time job at an interactive advertising agency, she freelances for publishing houses and game companies. She has illustrated covers for over 20 titles and designed characters for four games. In her spare time, she enjoys music, art, good food, and fitness activities. To see more of Helen's work, visit: www.helen-huang.com or www.flickr.com/photos/helenhuangy.

Filip Komorowski

Filip "Papa" Komorowski is a typographer, designer, graffiti artist, and music producer in Warsaw, Poland. He studied graphic design and now works as a freelance typographer. He co-founded the Juicy Color Brand art collective and is a member of Jthree Concepts team. See more of his work at: www.behance.net/komorowski.

Bree Léman

Bree Léman draws her design inspiration from her travels, particularly in Europe, where she studies urban culture, contemporary fashion, and architecture. She earned a Bachelor of Fine Arts degree in illustration and graphic design from Moore College of Art and Design and worked as a freelancer artist for Metro Creative Graphics and My Bliss Magazine. She illustrated the children's book *Friends Are Like Shoes* (Tate Publishing, 2008). To see more of Bree's work, visit: www.breeleman.com and http://breeleman.deviantart.com.

Grelin Machin

Grelin Machin is an illustrator living in Montreal, where she's trying to build her little army of clowns. She has a bacc in graphic design, but she's more intrigued by illustration than anything else. She has a thing for vector art but also loves to work with wood and colored pencils. Find her work at: http://grelin-machin.deviantart.com and http://grelinmachin.tumblr.com.

Svetlana Makarova

Svetlana Makarova is a freelance fashion illustrator from Ukraine. Her work has been featured in the *Great Big Book of Fashion Illustration* by Martin Dawber (Batsford, 2011). To see more of Svetlana's work, visit: http://lanitta.com and http://lanitta.deviantart.com.

McKelly

Kate McInnes and Sean Kelly are the collaborative creative duo known as McKelly, based in Melbourne, Australia. Kate is Editor of Vectortuts and a founding member of Blood Sweat Vector. Sean is completing his Masters in animation and interactive media and teaching at RMIT University. Find out more at: www.mckelly.com.au.

Sharon Milne

Sharon Milne is an illustrator and writer living in the United Kingdom, and she is the curator of this book. See the About the Curator page for more about Sharon.

Jared Nickerson

Jared Nickerson is a self-taught illustrator and graphic designer based in Seattle, WA. The focus of his studio, Jthree Concepts, is branding, character, logo, videogame, editorial, and textile design. He also specializes in art direction and consulting. Jared is co-founder of the vector community Blood Sweat Vector (BSV). When he's not designing, Jared is working with his band, Dead Astronauts, and spending time with his wife and pugs. See more of his work at: http://j3concepts.deviantart.com and http://j3concepts.prosite.com.

Nastasia Peters

Nastasia Peters is an illustrator and writer. Having artists for parents, she had the opportunity to grow up learning about art and being encouraged to try her hand at it herself. See more of her work at: https://ssst.deviantart.com and https://www.facebook.com/nastasiapeters.

Ivan Petrushevski

Ivan Petrushevski works as a graphic designer and illustrator for an advertising agency. See more from him at: www.facebook.com/flimovski and http://ivan-bliznak.deviantart.com.

Cindel Ribbens

Cindel Ribbens is an illustrator and character designer. Find her portfolio at: http://cindelribbens.daportfolio.com.

Michelle Romo

Michelle Romo is a self-taught illustrator and designer who is fueled by cookies and naps. She is the artist behind the line of cute characters and products known as Crowded Teeth. She currently resides in Los Angeles with her husband Jason and their two cats, Hurts and Morgan. See more of her work at: www.crowded-teeth.deviantart.com, www.facebook.com/superfuncrowdedteeth, and www.twitter.com/monstromo.

Rian Saputra

Rian Saputra, also known as Ryannzha, is an illustrator, user interface designer, and art director working on mobile applications, and he is active on blogs and art communities across the web. To see more of Rian's work, visit www.ryannzha.deviantart.com.

Samuel Sinaga

Samuel Sinaga is an art director for an advertising agency as well as a freelance illustrator in Indonesia. He enjoys cuddling with his girlfriend, playing online games, and watching sci-fi movies. See more of his work at: www.flowisking.net and http://flowisking.deviantart.com.

Cristiano Siqueira

Cristiano Siqueira is an illustrator from São Paulo, Brazil, specializing in vector and digital illustration and working for clients around the world creating illustrations for magazines, book covers, T-shirts, and advertising. See more of his work at: http://crisvector.deviantart.com and www.crisvector.com.

Junichi Tsuneoka

Junichi Tsuneoka was born and raised in Japan. He founded Studio Stubborn Sideburn to broaden his visual communication and to employ his visual language in art, illustration, and design. See more from him at: twitter.com/stbnsdbn, https://www.facebook.com/stubbornsideburns, and www.behance.net/stubborn_sideburn.

Mary Winkler

Mary Winkler (aka Acrylicana) is a freelance illustrator with shoe and accessory lines in the United States. Her work is painted on canvas or a variety of papers, or printed by way of giclée inkjet or silk screen, usually onto fabric. Mary studied Illustration at College for Creative Studies in Detroit, Michigan. See more of her work at: https://twitter.com/acrylicana, https://www.facebook.com/AcrylicanaFans, and www.behance.net/acrylicana.

About the Curator

Sharon Milne grew up wanting to be a mathematics or art teacher, as she enjoyed both subjects. But with the advice of her high school career counselor, she embarked on other lines of work, including sales and human resources. Meanwhile, her interest in digital art forms began to flourish and in 2006 she became attracted to vector art and then Adobe Illustrator. She enjoyed creating vector art from stock images and adding small details, building up to stylized, detailed portraits; conceptual artwork; and quirky animal illustrations. She became an active member of the vector community, sharing the artwork of others to inspire, and also creating amateur tutorials for those just learning.

Her passion for teaching and being involved in the vector community didn't stop there, as she became a community volunteer for the largest art community on the Internet, deviantArt. She looked after the vector galleries. She took the role a step further and became a Community Volunteer Mentor, helping other volunteers enhance their experience to give back to the community. Then in March 2010 she was interviewed as an "Inspirational Artist" by one of the largest vector tutorial site on the Internet, Vectortuts+. The interviewer suggested she try writing tutorials professionally, and there began her relationship with Vectortuts+. On a regular basis she wrote freelance tutorials for the site and was able to quit her full-time job to take on writing about vector professionally, both in theory work and tutorials, as well as showcasing the talent of others in the community.

She began writing tutorials for other graphic design sites, including Noupe, Abduzeedo, and Adobe's own Illustrator blog. She began being represented with an illustration agency and did commercial illustrations as well as privately commissioned work. However, her true love was teaching others how to create vector art and the tools of Adobe Illustrator. In July 2012, she became the Associate Editor of Vectortuts+, where she's been able to get further involved with teaching and the vector community.

Sharon lives in the North East of England in a town called Morpeth with her partner, Paul. She's an avid animal lover and shares her life with two cats, Sameria and Harley Quinn, and Cavalier King Charles Spaniel, Shelley. Given the chance, she'd have plenty more! When she's not creating vector art (which she also enjoys as a hobby), she loves spending time with her family, playing computer games, listening to a wide variety of music, watching trash TV, and dying her hair a multitude of bright colors. Her creative idols include the pop artist Andy Warhol and drag queen RuPaul, both of which inspire her artwork.